Tarot
Unfolded

The Knight, Death, and the Devil. Engraving by Albrecht Dürer, 1513. All three are also cards of the Tarot. Death and the Devil belong to the Major Arcana, and there is a Knight in each of the four suits.

Tarot
Unfolded

Imaginative Reading of the Divination Cards

Stefan Stenudd

arriba.se

Stefan Stenudd is a Swedish author, historian of ideas, artist, and a long-time instructor in the peaceful martial art aikido. He has published a number of books in Swedish as well as English, both fiction and non-fiction.

Among the latter are interpretations of the Chinese classic *Tao Te Ching* and the Japanese samurai classic *Go Rin no Sho* by Miyamoto Musashi. His novels explore existential subjects from Stone Age drama to science fiction, but lately stay more and more focused on the present. He has also written some plays for the stage and the screen. In the history of ideas he studies the thought patterns of creation myths, as well as Aristotle's *Poetics*. He has his own extensive website:
www.stenudd.com

Also by Stefan Stenudd:
Tao Te Ching. The Taoism of Lao Tzu Explained, 2011.
Cosmos of the Ancients. The Greek Philosophers on Myth and Cosmology, 2007, 2011.
Life Energy Encyclopedia, 2009.
Your Health in Your Horoscope. Introduction to Medical Astrology, 2009.
Aikido Principles, 2008.
Qi. Increase Your Life Energy, 2008.
Attacks in Aikido, 2008.
Aikibatto. Sword Exercises for Aikido Students, 2007.

Fiction:
Occasionally I Contemplate Murder, 2006, 2011.
All's End, 2007.

Tarot Unfolded: Imaginative Reading of the Divination Cards.
Copyright © Stefan Stenudd, 2012.
Cover and book design by the author.
All rights reserved.
ISBN 978-91-7894-055-4
Publisher: Arriba, Malmö, Sweden, info@arriba.se
www.arriba.se

Contents

Preface

I was introduced to the Tarot cards in my early twenties, by a friend who was quite learned about all kinds of divination methods. It was love at first sight. The charming illustrations on each of the cards, full of symbolism and intriguing mystery, were a feast for my eyes and got my imagination roaming behind them.

The Tarot works by images, as do we humans to a great extent. Words make us wonder, numbers puzzle us, but images make immediate impressions on our minds, at lightning speed. They dance with our dreams, play with our memories, and blend with our perception of the world we live in. We are creatures of imagination. As the word suggests, that's mainly done by images, swirling in our minds.

So, reading the Tarot cards is processing the images in our imagination. We get it to the extent we allow ourselves to think in pictures, and that comes naturally to us all.

That's why I dared to choose the ambiguous subtitle for this book. "Imaginative reading" suggests mere fantasy. Maybe so. Lots of people would claim that's all it is. But fantasy is no trifle. It's how we relate to the world and its many enigmas. It gives us ideas by which we are able to discover the secrets of the universe. It unfolds reality.

I can't think of any other human capacity that takes us farther than fantasy has done through the past thousands of years, and continues to do. It's the fuel of creativity, and what surpasses the ability to create?

Therefore, whether we put trust in the divinations or not, reading the Tarot cards through our imagination inspires us to reconsider what we are, where we are, and the constantly elusive answer to the question why. Perhaps the wondrous way our mind relates to what is called reality will present some dazzling revelations along the way – or at the very least some thought provoking surprises.

Although I've played with the Tarot on numerous occasions through the years, I never thought of writing a book about it. Going from pictures to letters seems like retreating. But then it hit me that this was exactly what I felt like talking about: Reading the Tarot is taking in the images and letting them show themselves, unbound by words and reason. Our imagination will do the rest, and the result has its very own profundity. A picture is worth a thousand words.

So, in the following I will try to tickle the imagination of the reader into going on the spiritual quest induced by imagery. See the Tarot pictures come alive and make other pictures emerge from your mind to meet and transform them. It's like going to the movies. It's what we do.

If you haven't indulged in it before, you may find that the world will never look the same again.

Stefan Stenudd
July, 2012

Tarot
Fundamentals

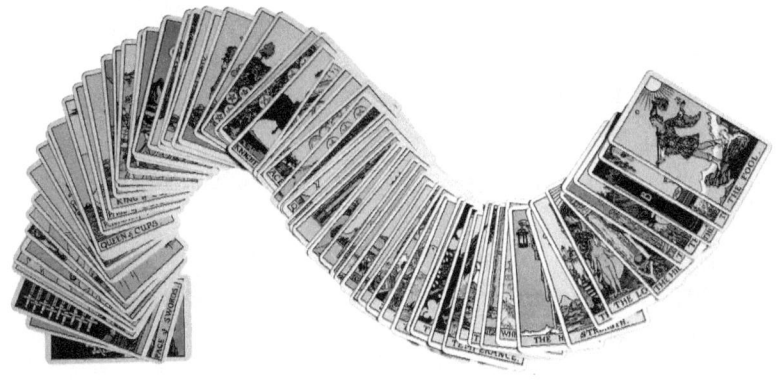

Nine versions of the Tarot card The Fool.

Introduction

Tarot is the extended deck of cards, usually 78, used for divination. The cards are laid out in a spread where each card represents an aspect of the future or a significant circumstance about the present. It's an old tradition, dating back to the Renaissance.

Playing cards are originally a Chinese invention, documented already in the 9th century, but the actual Tarot appeared in Europe around 1440, also at first for card games. The European use of the decks for divination, *cartomancy*, commenced in the 16th century and grew during the following centuries. That's just about the only use of the Tarot deck today, and it has become widely spread.

Alongside the Tarot, though, other decks of cards were developed mainly for the purpose of card games. The standard playing card deck today has 52 cards in four suits of 13 cards each. In some games a Joker is added, but that's a much later invention.

The Tarot's link to the playing cards is evident in the division into four suits, although their names differ slightly. But the Tarot has 14 cards in each suit, adding a Page to the court cards. These 56 cards in total are called the Minor Arcana. More importantly, the Tarot has 22 trump cards called the Major Arcana, separate from the

The Magician from nine Tarot decks through the centuries.

four suits. They represent universal powers or symbols of a higher magnitude than the four suits.

Because of the distant past of the Tarot card deck, there are many variations existing alongside one another today. The cards vary slightly in names, imagery, numbers, et cetera, but no more than that they are easily compared.

Since I was first introduced to the Tarot in the 1970's, I use the Rider-Waite Tarot deck, which is by far the most popular one in the world today. It's my favorite, too – until I find the time to make my own version, which is what I really recommend for everyone who finds delight in divination with a Tarot deck. That's how to perfect it.

Divination by Images

It must be understood that the Tarot cards work by images, especially the Rider-Waite deck, which has descriptive images for all the 78 cards. And that's the thing.

Since the Renaissance, cards were decorated with allegorical images, carrying lots of symbolic meanings familiar to people at the time. When they saw these images, their minds went spinning on how to interpret them in relation to the question at hand. That's still the best way to work with the Tarot cards.

Any card deck with a number of images that are meaningful and suggestive to the viewer will inspire an enlightening reading. Watch the pictures and let your mind spin.

That's why, ultimately, you need to make your own deck with the images to which you relate the most, the ones that make you react and get your imagination going. Maybe you can use your photo album, or search the internet for pictures you find significant – somewhat like the old tradition of collecting material for a scrapbook.

Until then, I recommend that you work with the Rider-Waite deck, which has wonderfully suggestive images on all the 78 Tarot cards – although these pictures are evidently from an era other than ours.

These Tarot cards were originally published in the

The first four cards of the Rider-Waite Pentacles suit.

beginning of the 20th century, and it shows. The style of the drawings is charming, as if for children's fairy-tales even when the motifs are far from childish. But the imagery is also full of references to the 19th century occultism of which A. E. Waite, the mastermind behind the deck, was part.

These components add to the intrigue of the card deck, but they also narrow down its applicability to the mentality and society of our time. Just like the old classics need to be translated anew as time passes and civilization changes, we probably need new Tarot imagery every now and then, so that the pictures speak to us in ways to which we can relate.

Therefore, optimally, you need a Tarot deck of your own making, or at the very least you must carefully pick one that you relate to with ease.

In this book you find several examples of different Tarot card decks through the centuries. Quite a few have been added these last decades, although I'm yet to see one with which I wouldn't hesitate to replace the Rider-Waite deck.

Don Quixote, swept away by his imagination, surrounding him with all kinds of creatures from the books he reads with such empathy. Illustration by Gustave Doré, 1863.

The World of the Imagination

The human mind is incredible. It opens the universe to us. It reveals all that is real and creates what is not. It even makes us aware of ourselves, which is probably its most marvelous feats. Certainly, it also plays tricks on us.

The foremost instrument we have for dealing with the world we live in is the imaginary world we have within. We experience it intensely and use it constantly, thereby finding our way where our bodies wander. But it doesn't exist. It's like a parallel universe of the kind astronomers today speculate about. It's here and now, but has no contact at all with the universe mapped by the astronomers.

Well, in the case of the world within our minds, we are the points of contact, the borders and links between inner and outer existence. The two worlds flow through us and influence one another with us as their tools.

Events of the outer world change our impression of it, which changes the imaginary world we cultivate within. But that inner world also contains what we wish of the outside world, so we do our best to change the latter accordingly. As civilization advances, we get so much better at it, occasionally it's to our own disadvantage.

Whatever the final outcome, if there is one, we can't stop. The inner world moves at least as much as the outer one does, and there's no break that we know of. Ever

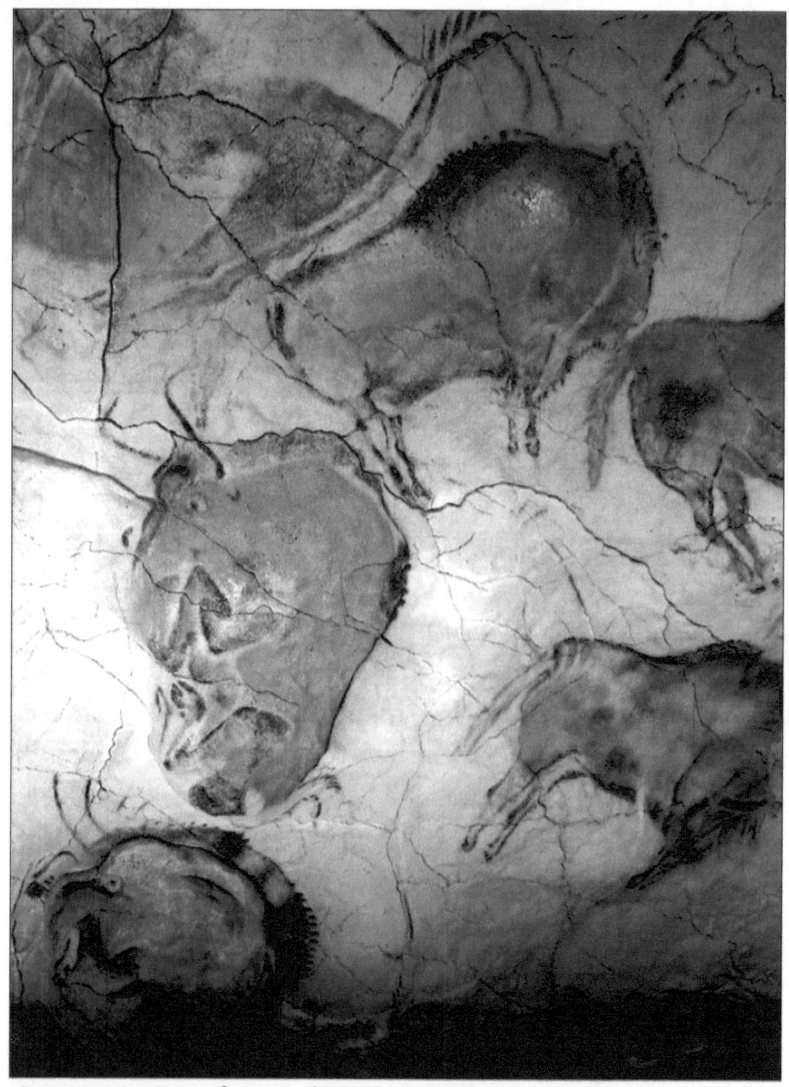

Cave paintings from Altamira, Spain, circa 15,000 – 30,000 years old, discovered in 1879. The authenticity of these cave paintings was at first questioned by the scientific community, doubting that people were capable of any artistic expression that long ago. We're unwise to assume that our ancestors were intellectually impaired, when they had brains as big as ours.

since our brains began to grow way past the volume of other primates, it started galloping. That was two million years ago.

It's hard to exaggerate how much primordial man must have marveled at what kept appearing from inside his mind, in the form of fantasies and dreams. He was caught between two enigmas – that of the outside world, with its incomprehensible mechanisms, and that of the inner world, seemingly endless and frequently chaotic. Only by trying to somehow match the two worlds would he find his place in them. To the extent they could be made to coexist without absurdity ensuing, man's life quality improved.

But the inner world is a wild beast, comparable to those predators primordial man struggled to escape. Images appearing from within could be just as bewildering and frightening at times, often making even less sense than what was perceived in the outside world.

Still, very often these enigmas were related, in so much as the fantasies were the mind's way of trying to make sense of the surrounding world. That was not easy without the scientific knowledge we have today. Well, it still isn't. Primordial man would be just as puzzled when trying to figure out his inner world by regarding the outside world as a clue to it.

And then there are dreams.

What could primordial man possibly have concluded about those sleep worlds, appearing just as real as the outside world, but even less controllable. There, the impossible seemed to make sense. Even persons who were long

The Dream. Painting by Henri Rousseau, 1910.

gone participated as if having returned unharmed from death, alongside others who were utter strangers and still were dealt with as longtime friends. Nothing could be taken for granted, from one moment to the next.

What evolved, as a defense and an effort to explain all these absurdities of the inner as well as the outer world, was myth.

Myth and Archetypes

Most of what we call myth was originally speculation in an effort to explain the world and all its dazzling phenomena. It was a process in which imagination assembled the inner world with the outer, sort of like a jigsaw puzzle. When the images that were formed made some sense in both worlds, they were kept and expanded all the way to complete cosmologies.

The formation of myth was a kind of research. Myths that helped people relate to their reality became trusted and were orally transmitted from generation to generation, until they were written down – if not replaced by other myths along the way, and forgotten.

So, myths have their own evolutionary law, their own survival of the fittest. Those that gain trust are enforced, also improved as human experience increases. The ones that for one reason or other become less convincing will be discarded. Their purpose is to shed some light on what to make of it all.

Some elements and themes came rather naturally, because of what could be observed already by primordial man. Dreams made him aware of something existing apart from the palpable world his body inhabited. So, myths emerged about what existed beyond and around what the eyes could see.

The Fall, from Genesis II, the second creation story of the Bible. Note that the serpent in the tree still has arms, not yet punished by God. The Garden of Eden is full of animals living in peace. The couple in the background at the left is surely an image of Adam and Eve in the innocent happiness they had before they bit the apple from the Tree of Knowledge. The idea of some or other knowledge stolen from the gods is common in creation myths. Often it's not knowledge, but fire. Painting by Cornelis van Haarlem, 1592.

People died, but were remembered as clearly as if they still walked beside their survivors. So, there were myths to explain what had become of them, because they clearly had not disappeared completely even after their bodies decayed into dust.

And people were born out of the bellies of their mothers, soon growing just as big as them. Myths were needed to explain it. Also, during their lives, fate struck people very differently, rewarding some tremendously and striking down hard on others. Again, myths were made to explain it.

The earthly life and its burdens raised numerous questions. So did the sky high above their heads. The sun with its warmth and light appeared and disappeared daily, whereas the moon moved differently and its light was as cold as it was weak in comparison. Not only that, but in the cluster of little white dots on the night sky, some moved and the others did not. Myths took care of that.

The greatest mystery of all was from where it all came.

Had there been a beginning, and if so, what caused it? One woman out of whose womb the first child fell – but if so, where did that woman come from? One man, whose seed had planted that first child in its mother's womb – but again, where would that man have come from? One first morning enlightened by the sun, but out of what did the sun originally emerge?

This was the greatest challenge for myth to meet, and many myths did. Some did it well enough to survive for thousands of years. A few of them are still around.

The birth of Venus, the goddess of love, also the name given to one of the planets. In many cultures around the world, the planets have been regarded as deities. Painting by Sandro Botticelli, 1485.

Some of these myths, but not as many as one might think, also dealt with the possible future end of it all.

When watching myths as ancient explanations to the mysteries of life, patterns become clear. In all the cultures and eras we have been able to study, myths of old form systems of explanations for worldly life as the human mind experiences it.

Whatever primordial man wondered about, could be dealt with in a myth. So, their number increased, as did their complexity. They gave solace and a comforting feeling of life making sense. This was a need of the mind, satisfied by the very capacity of the mind that created the need.

The four horsemen of the Apocalypse, bringing death, famine, war, and plague, as told by the Book of Revelations, ending the New Testament with a vision of the end of the world as we know it. Far from all mythologies have a story about how the world will end. Woodcut by Albrecht Dürer, 1498.

The god Saturn devouring one of his children, in the primordial chaotic time described by Greek and Roman myths, when gods were at war among themselves. Painting by Francisco Goya, 1823.

Archetypes

Myths have themes. They are stories dealing with specific subjects, the roots of which have been described above. But stories also have characters, and in the case of myths they are often representing much more than a single person doing this or that at a whim or from some basic human need. They are not just types, but archetypes.

It's a term from Ancient Greece, signifying what we would call a prototype, a model on which other things are based. It doesn't necessarily refer to characters in a play. Plato meant that behind the real world, there are ideal forms from which our world finds its shapes.

The use of the term archetype for myth and drama was made popular by the psychoanalyst C. G. Jung, who presented his application of it in 1919. He found patterns in folklore, myth, and art, from which he extracted several symbolical types, characters carrying certain meanings, which could be explained as different aspects of the human mentality.

He claimed that these archetypes are the same through history and in every culture, almost as if included in the human genome. By studying the archetypes and their meanings, we can learn to understand ourselves.

That can be discussed. The patterns he found might instead have been those of characters and roles necessary in drama, with which mankind has been occupied for thousands of years. Some of the archetypes are easily recognized from the recurring characters in drama history: the king, the mother, the sage, the hero, the villain, and so on.

An angel stops Abraham from sacrificing his son Isaac to God. Three archetypes (or four, including God) in a drama similar to that of many other myths. Painting by Rembrandt van Rijn, 1634.

Leda seduced by the god Zeus in the shape of a swan. A myth popular among artists as well as psychologists, but for different reasons. The theme of forbidden love is about as frequent in myth as it is in reality. Painting by Peter Paul Rubens, c. 1600.

It's a bit like the chicken or the egg, though. Jung would have claimed that the archetypes were there before the drama, which had to incorporate them in order to enthrall the audience. Indeed, drama as well as literature carried the insights of psychology long before the science of it was invented.

An anthropologist might remind us that human life revolves around certain social roles, ever since we got this gargantuan brain of ours. There are mothers, fathers, and children. There are also leaders, advisors, priests, warriors,

Again a mythological seduction: Ganymede abducted by Zeus, taken to Olympus where he was to serve as a cup-bearer. In Greek mythology, humans were handled with little care by the gods. This, too, is a painting by Peter Paul Rubens, from 1612.

heroes and cowards, followers and agitators, artists, dreamers, wanderers, hunters, lovers, and so on and so forth. Each one of us has bits and pieces of it all.

Anyway, the idea of the archetype is as interesting in psychology as it is in drama. Myth, it seems, is full of them, the larger than life characters proudly carrying their sharply chiseled traits. Those who really excel at their archetypes are usually called gods in the myths.

If we extract the archetypes from a myth or a play, we see the plot more clearly and understand their actions better. We also become aware of the patterns by which life tends to repeat itself whenever and wherever. The human condition can be described through archetypes, which are necessities by which our actions and our sentiments are governed.

For example, any child can find that the dependency of the mother may become a burden of which one needs to rid oneself, and the admiration of the father easily becomes a rivalry of sorts, maybe even contempt at length. It's part of growing up. That's also the core of what Jung meant the archetypes to be: clues to self-realization.

A leader is sort of the father of fathers, and the leader of leaders we call god, whether imagined or not. A hero is what we want to be, but we can't if the hero we look up to is constantly guarding our safety, doing the heroic deeds for us. An adversary angers us, but would we ever move an inch if not confronted by one? And no adversary is more persistent than the one each of us carries in our mind. A lover is sweet, but never as sweet as when we are the reciprocal object of that love. And how easily love turns into the opposite!

Indeed, there are patterns by which we live, and as Shakespeare said:

All the world's a stage
And all the men and women merely players
They have their exits and their entrances
And one man in his time plays many parts.

The great red dragon and the beast from the sea, two of the many horrifying creatures described in the Book of Revelations. Watercolour by William Blake, 1805. There's a myriad of monsters in the myths, most of them carrying archetype traits.

We're not allowed to read the whole script beforehand, although divination takes a crack at it, but we do well to get familiar with the characters, especially the one – or the ones – we ourselves must play.

Tarot Archetypes

In divination, the idea of archetypes is instrumental, and used in abundance. That's true also for what can be described as the mother of all divination: astrology. The twelve signs of the Zodiac, with their distinct characteristics, are archetypes. So are the planets, having the names of deities.

It's just as true for the Tarot. Each of the 78 cards can be seen as a kind of archetype. It's the most evident with the 22 cards of the Major Arcana, representing central principles, mostly in personalized forms: the Fool, the Magician, the Empress, the Devil, the Hermit, and so on. Later in this book, I describe their archetypical traits in more detail.

In a Tarot reading, as well as in readings with ordinary playing cards, it's common to understand a character image on the card as someone significant that you will meet. That can happen, but it's not necessarily the case.

What the card is really showing is that the archetype in question will be relevant in your life, either in the form of a certain person appearing or in some other way that has the characteristics of the archetype.

For example, the Fool might mean that you meet somebody who is hard to take seriously, but generally speaking it suggests that something will happen or appear

The twelve signs of the Zodiac. From Leopoldus: Compilatio de astrorum scientia, 1489.

that you do best to treat in a casual manner. Depending on the position of the card in the spread, it can also mean that you are not taken seriously, although you feel you should be. Or the turn of events is such that you can do little more than shrug your shoulders and say: "That's life."

A king or a queen in the spread doesn't necessarily

mean that you will have to deal with a certain person of power, but it does imply that you need to tread carefully, because there are powers superior to yours involved. On the other hand, in another position, the card can suggest that you need to act like a king or a queen.

If you take the habit of treating each card as sort of an archetype, carrying a certain trait that needs to be considered, your reading will be much clearer than if you immediately search for specifics.

Life is complicated. We need to generalize aspects of it to be able to make decisions, choose between our options, and move on. The archetypes of the Tarot are excellent generalizations of common ingredients in life. Those cards that appear in a spread show what ingredients are particularly relevant and important in regard to the question on which your reading is based.

Let you imagination go. It will easily find what circumstances would be accurately described by the archetypes appearing in the cards. That's why they are archetypes – they can be found everywhere, and they do make sense. But that's only if you take it in and trust your imagination, instead of consulting a manual specifying exactly what each card decides about your future.

Another illuminating method is to regard the cards as principles: the principle of the Knight of Swords, who bravely hurries to battle against any foe, the principle of the Lovers, who forget everything else when facing each other, the principle of the Hermit, who seeks solitude whatever others might root for, et cetera. The principle is simply the core of an archetype, the meaning it carries.

The Last Judgment. This biblical myth, or vision, is implied by the Tarot card The Judgment of the Major Arcana. Fresco from the Sistine Chapel by Michelangelo, 1541.

Also the structure of myth is applicable to Tarot readings. The myth is a story involving a number of archetypes interacting. The Tarot spread is also a story, told by several cards in a certain order. So, you have to find how this story makes sense, how one thing leads to another in a way that almost seems unavoidable.

The Judgment card (archaically spelled 'Judgement') of the Rider-Waite Tarot deck.

The past leads through the present into the future. Looking at the past, you should understand why the present is as it is. That also means you can get a good idea of what comes next. The cards help you through this mental process and give you the clues to make it more accurate than you would have done without them, simply because life is so complicated, every moment so confusing. Without a systematic approach, it's chaos.

If you can make the Tarot reading like telling a story, from the beginning to the end, with characters and events making some kind of sense all through, then you manage fine and need no further study, only practice. Practice makes perfect.

The perspective of the myth, and the archetypes populating it, also reminds us of the basic fact that nothing is really new under the sun. The important and fundamental parts of what happens to us have happened to countless people before, and to a surprisingly high extent in much the same way.

Allegory of Time unveiling Truth. An allegory is the artistic way of representing principles and ideas by persons and objects, much like the concept of archetypes. Painting by Jean François de Troy, 1733.

Not that it solves every problem and dissolves any worry. It's new when it happens to us.

But it's far from unique. There is previous experience to learn from. Divination by the Tarot or any other method connects us to the source and essence of all that previous experience – if we open up and trust the only means by which this source becomes available to us. That's our imagination.

The Tarot Speaks to You

To some extent it can be said about most methods of divination, but it's particularly true about the Tarot: It speaks directly to the one making the reading. The cards seemingly picked by chance are those that the reader will interpret in the proper way.

This may seem like stating the obvious, but it has important implications. Since the Tarot speaks through images, the interpretation of them is done differently depending on what eyes are watching and the mind behind them processing those images.

Each of us is equipped with what can be called a context of our own. Talents, emotions, thoughts, beliefs, experiences and conclusions made by them – all of those things make up our mentality and influence how we perceive the world around us. When we see the Tarot cards, we will see them differently, maybe just slightly so, but in some cases the difference can be as big as between two languages.

This uncertainty between how individuals see images can be compared to what the philosopher Ludwig Wittgenstein in his later work called language-games, where he stated that there is little to tell us that we ever mean the same thing when using the same word. That is even truer when it comes to pictures, which are virtually impossible to define in an objective way.

Let's take one example. The 15th card of the Tarot's Major Arcana is The Devil, showing him like a demon crouching on a pedestal to which man and woman are chained, completely naked.

THE DEVIL.

The image is full of Judeo-Christian symbols, such as the Devil of the Bible as well as Adam and Eve, the horns on their heads suggesting their fall into sin.

A conservative Christian would find the card one of horror, warning about how easily man falls for temptation and the eternal slavery it leads to. To such a mind the card seems like the symbol of pure evil.

Somebody with an occultist background, on the other hand, may see it as encouragement to challenge obsolete values and free oneself from the chains they put on us. Like Lou Reed expressed it: "Take a walk on the wild side." Many artists would probably think along somewhat the same line, convinced that without defiance there is no art and no progress.

Someone versed in psychoanalytical terminology would think of libido and the way we humans tend to mix lust with guilt. If so, the card seems to show how fear and inhibition stops us from pursuing our path and realizing our potential. Those who are raised strictly and stick to Victorian morals would instead see the image as one of

Mars and Venus discovered by the gods. The joining of the gods of war and love must indeed have been surprising also to the gods, but as archetypes they have always been related. In the Roman myth, their child was Cupid, the god of desire. Painting by Joachim Wtewael, 1604.

carnal desire and its dreadful consequences to one's character.

A lawyer might see it as a reminder of the necessity of law, or all hell breaks loose. An atheist might find it hard to relate to the card in any other way than as a joke. And those billions of people with an upbringing outside the Judeo-Christian cultures would need a manual to relate at all to the picture. They might guess that it shows man and woman as children of the beast – or food for him, chained like cattle before the slaughter.

What we see in images depends on what images we already have in our heads.

So, to use the Tarot properly it must be understood that the one doing the reading is the one the images of the cards speak to. That's true also if the reading is done for somebody else. The reader is the interpreter, so the images have to relate correctly to that person's internal imagery. And they do, in a mysterious way.

Therefore, when you make a reading, don't worry about what the "true" meaning of a card might be. No manual can compete with your intuition, since you are the one making the spread and reading it. If you have one impression of a card and a manual suggest another – trust yourself more. That's so to speak what the Tarot is doing, and serving you the cards accordingly.

Of course, this is also true about the meanings I suggest for the 78 Tarot cards later in this book. They are mere suggestions, really only intended to trigger your own imagination into doing all the work. You have to take the images in and extract their messages from the tur-

Gilgamesh with a captured lion. Bas-relief from Khorsabad, 8th century BC. The Epic of Gilgamesh, from Mesopotamia, can be traced back some 4,000 years, making it one of the oldest remaining texts. This hero king struggles in several ways with death, even trying to return his companion Enkidu from it. He finally learns to accept death, in spite of its horrors.

moil that is your mentality, experience, and acquired life wisdom. That's a reading worth contemplating.

From the above follows that each reader of a Tarot spread will get different cards for the same question (as chance would have it). That's because they read them differently, but also because their reading is done from their perspective and the answers will be restricted to it. Life is so complex that there is more than one answer to any question – each dealing with different aspects of the question and with separate facets of the answer.

You can experiment with this by trying one and the same question with a friend who is also familiar with the Tarot. Each of you makes a spread and reads it. Then you compare. So as not to make one reading influence the next, you should do them without the other person present and compare them only when that's done. You'll find that both readings have their merits.

Maybe that's the very core of any divination technique: it's nourished by the wisdom and experience of the reader.

Tarot
Decks

The Major Arcana of the Rider-Waite Tarot deck.

The Rider-Waite Tarot Card Deck

By far the most famous and widely used Tarot card deck today is the one called Rider-Waite. It was published in 1909 and has been reprinted countless times since.

The Rider-Waite Tarot card deck was designed by the occult writer Arthur Edward Waite (1857-1942) and the artist Pamela Colman Smith (1878-1951). Rider was the name of the original publisher.

It's a charming work with great attention to detail. A. E. Waite (see the photo) was a learned occultist, so he made sure that all possible symbols and archetypical settings were included. Pamela Colman Smith made her illustrations according to his instructions, but also with a sweet artistic spirit, as if making pictures for a wonderful fairytale.

Contrary to most other decks, especially the old ones, the Rider-Waite Tarot deck has pictures on every card, each image representing a sentiment or a situation. That makes divination with them so much easier and a lot more fun. It creates a reading based on images and our impressions of them, which is something almost unique to Tarot.

I wholeheartedly recommend it. Although there are websites with all the 78 Tarot cards of the deck online and methods to make readable spreads of them, there's something inimitable about holding the actual cards in your hands, shuffling them, and arranging them on a table. If you want to try Tarot more than once, you must get the deck – so to speak IRL.

Tarot Cards Through the Centuries

The Tarot cards emerged in the 15th century, around 1440 to be more precise, initially as playing cards. They have taken many shapes through the centuries. On the following pages are some of the most famous ones.

The invention of playing cards was Chinese and happened at least as far back as the 9th century. The European use of the decks for divination, *cartomancy*, commenced in the 16th century and grew during the following centuries. By time, the differences between playing cards and Tarot divination cards increased.

Variations on the theme of the latter multiplied – to no surprise, since the imaginative imagery of the Tarot practically insists on personal creativity. We will surely have more of them in the future.

That's fortunate. Each time and each culture has its own imagery and its own impression of pictures. Innovation is what makes sure that new generations can relate to the imagery.

The odd thing is that old Tarot decks keep on being reprinted as well. So it seems that some things never change.

Charles VI Tarot

One of the oldest Tarot card decks remaining is the one called Charles VI after a French king, although it was made in Italy – and well after his death. It was hand-painted by an unknown artist in the late 15th century.

The cards are gold plated, so if not for a king they were obviously made for a client with considerable means. Only 17 of the cards remain, whereof all but one are from the Major Arcana. Here are twelve of them.

Visconti-Sforza Tarot

Another old Tarot card deck, also from the 15th century, is that of Visconti and Sforza, named after the Italian noblemen for whom the deck was made.

It's actually a number of decks, none of them remaining complete. Here are twelve cards from the Major Arcana of one of those decks.

Tarot of Marseille

The Tarot of Marseille is a standard design for Tarot cards, given the name in the 19th century by the French occultist Papus. The name simply refers to many cards of this design being produced in Marseille for hundreds of years. Its imagery suggests a Renaissance origin.

The design is similar to that of traditional Italian Tarot cards, and that was where France got it from. The cards are still produced in this fixed and recognizable style.

The twelve Major Arcana cards here are from the Jean Dodal deck, produced 1701-1715, but the design was mainly kept the same through the centuries. It still is.

Tarot of Etteilla

The first Tarot deck designed specifically for divination use was that of Etteilla, created around 1788. Etteilla was born Jean-Baptiste Alliette (1738-91), but reversed his name when entering the occultist profession. He may have been the first professional Tarot reader, also getting very successful with it.

In his Tarot he combined symbols of ancient Egypt, astrology, and other esoteric material floating around at his time. His work and theories had a lot of influence on the occultists to come in the following centuries. For example, it's easy to see many links between Etteilla's Tarot and that of Rider-Waite.

Etteilla's Tarot deck has been printed in many slightly different designs. Here are twelve of the Major Arcana cards of the original design, although from a late 19th century printing.

Rider-Waite Tarot

The Rider-Waite Tarot card deck, presented earlier, was produced in 1909, but has been reproduced countless times since. It's the deck I use in this book.

It has rich imagery on all the cards, contrary to just about all previous decks. These images are full of symbols from the occultism of the time.

For easy comparison of style with the other decks presented, here is the Major Arcana of Rider-Waite again.

THE FOOL. THE WORLD. THE MOON.

THE TOWER. THE DEVIL. DEATH.

THE HANGED MAN. WHEEL of FORTUNE. THE HERMIT.

Unfolded

Thoth Tarot

Another occultist of the early 20th century was Aleister Crowley, who became the most famous of them all – and still is. He cooperated with the artist Frieda Harris to make his own version of the Tarot.

The project took five years, ending in 1943, but the deck was not printed until 1969.

As usual with what he worked on, Crowley fearlessly changed names on cards, even on one of the suits – turning Pentacles into Discs. The images are crowded with symbols from many occult and non-occult traditions.

Here are twelve of the Thoth Tarot Major Arcana cards.

 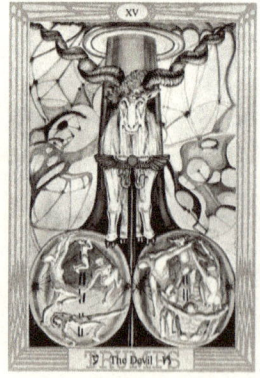 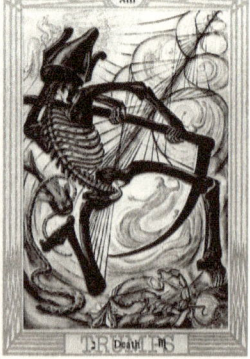

Hermetic Tarot

Both Waite and Crowley were connected to the Golden Dawn occultist order. That goes for Godfrey Dowson, too. He was the creator of the Hermetic Tarot, completed in the mid-1970's.

He made the originals in pen and ink, filling the images with symbols of alchemy, astrology, and Quabalah. It's intentionally made in black and white, which adds to the drama of the images.

Here are twelve of the Hermetic Tarot Major Arcana cards.

Magus of the Voice of Light   Children of the Voice Divine   The Magus of Power

The Foolish Man · 0 · The Spirit of Ether

Universe · XXI · The Great One of the Night of Time

The Last Judgment · XX · The Spirit of the Primal Fire

The Moon · XVIII · Ruler of Flux and Reflux

The Blasted Tower · XVI · Lord of the Hosts of the Mighty

The Devil · XV · Lord of the Gates of Matter

Death · XIII · Child of the Great Transformers

The Hanged Man · XII · Spirit of the Mighty Waters

The Wheel of Fortune · X · Lord of the Forces of Life

Unfolded

63

Aquarian Tarot

The Aquarian Tarot card deck was created by the American illustrator David Palladini, and published in 1970. The name, popular in the era of the deck's creation, refers to the astrological Age of Aquarius, which is to come after the present Age of Pisces. It has become a central concept in the New Age movement.

The Tarot deck illustrations are not that 1960's in style, though, but compare much more readily to Art Deco and poster art from the end of the 19th century, such as that of Mucha. Palladini's deck seems not to have been designed with a certain philosophy or occult teaching in mind.

Here are twelve of the Aquarian Tarot Major Arcana cards.

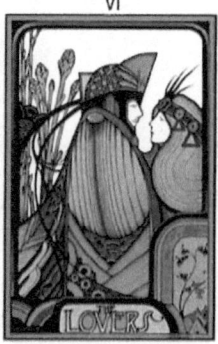

Mythic Tarot

In 1986, Liz Greene and Juliet Sharman-Burke developed the Mythic Tarot, inspired by Jungian symbolism and psychoanalysis. Like C. G. Jung, they lean heavily on Greek myth as material for their version.

Liz Greene is a famous astrologer and psychologist. Jung regarded the Tarot cards as examples of archetypes of transformation, something central in his depth psychology theories. This deck is intended to be used in line with that, as an instrument of self-development. The images give the impression of being illustrations of fairytales, which is to no surprise in this context.

Here are twelve of the cards from the Mythic Tarot Major Arcana.

THE LOVERS

THE HIEROPHANT

THE MAGICIAN

THE FOOL   THE WORLD   THE HERMIT

THE SUN   THE MOON   THE TOWER

THE DEVIL   DEATH   THE HANGED MAN

Unfolded

Tarot vs. Playing Cards

Tarot is the extended deck of cards, usually 78, used for divination, whereas the modern playing card deck has 52 regular cards – Jokers excluded. These two types of decks have the same roots, which are actually Chinese.

The playing card is a Chinese invention, documented already in the 9th century. The actual Tarot appeared in Europe around 1440, also at first for card games. Our modern deck of playing cards has the same origin.

By time the two decks developed differently, each according to its use. The use of cards for divination, *cartomancy*, commenced already in the 16th century and grew during the following centuries. That's just about the only use today of the Tarot deck, whereas playing cards are sometimes used for divination but mostly for card games.

Major and Minor Arcana

The Tarot deck is divided into two groups of cards – the Major Arcana of 22 cards and the Minor Arcana (also called Lesser Arcana) of 56 cards. The Minor Arcana is divided into four suits: Wands, Pentacles, Cups, and Swords, with 14 cards in each suit.

The playing card deck is almost the same as the Tarot Minor Arcana, but with four cards missing: the Page of each suit. The playing card deck and Tarot share the

The four pages of the Tarot, missing in the playing card deck.

Knight (Jack), Queen, and King, but Tarot also has a Page. Therefore there are only 52 playing cards, but 56 in the Minor Arcana.

Actually, there's one more card from the Tarot remaining in the playing card deck, which usually includes a Joker, although it's rarely used in card games. Its Tarot equivalent is from the Major Arcana: the Fool.

There's no historic evidence of the two having the same origin, though. The Joker was introduced in the USA in the 1850's, as a wild card or a trump. Still, their similarities are probably not pure coincidence.

The suits

In the original Chinese version of playing cards, each of the four suits dealt with money and riches – just more and more of them: coins, strings of coins, myriads (10,000) of coins, and tens of myriads of coins. That's a lot of coins.

The European versions, though, have come to spread over other subjects as well, incorporating typical allegorical motifs and themes that can be found in many examples of traditional symbolic thinking.

Since there are four suits, they have unavoidably been compared to the four elements of Ancient Greece: fire, earth, air, and water. This cosmological quartet has been of such influence since the time of the Greek philosophers that the suits of the Tarot card deck were made to conform to it.

Chinese playing cards.

Another influence is that of the four feudal classes: the military (aristocracy), the clergy, the merchants (trade), and the peasants (agriculture).

Wands or Clubs

The first of the suits is called Wands in the Tarot and Clubs in the playing card deck. Of the Greek elements, they represent earth – things concrete and earthbound. The life of the peasant. That might be why it's the suit regarded as the lowest also in many card games.

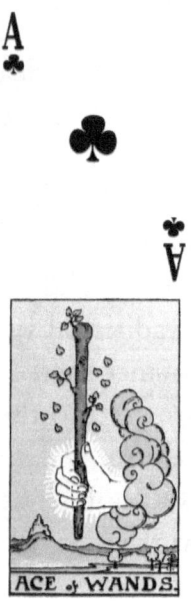

ACE of WANDS.

In some texts on the Tarot, Wands and Clubs are linked to the element fire, which makes no sense at all. It must be a modern modification of the allegorical thinking of the past, made to fit some system or other. There is little, if anything, in the Greek idea of the element fire to support this connection. Wands, as well as agriculture, belong to the element earth.

Pentacles or Diamonds

The second suit in the Tarot is that of Pentacles, equivalent to Diamonds of the playing card deck. This suit is the one where the Chinese origin is preserved the most. It's about riches, which is why it's surprising that the suit is not counted as the top one in either Tarot or playing card

ACE of PENTACLES

games. It suggests that the attitude towards wealth differs between ancient China and Europe.

Surely, Christianity has a role in this, since its message is that it's more difficult for the rich to enter Heaven than for the camel to pass through a needle's eye. Wealth is no virtue in the Christian tradition, but it sort of is in Chinese culture, where some regard it as a sign of being in accord with the Way of Heaven and receiving the award for it.

The Greek element corresponding to this suit is air, although it takes a bit of a stretch of the imagination. Air is about thought, communication, and mental processes in general. Ideas are jewels, certainly, and without them there is little chance of amassing a great fortune if not inheriting it. But everybody also knows that no fortune is as fortunate as wisdom, so there's the more direct link between the symbolic concepts.

Some texts link this suit to the Greek element earth, which makes some sense since money in our eyes is part of the material world. But that's a modern understanding of riches as well as of the element earth. In the past, the latter was closely linked to agriculture, working the soil, and the former was connected to aristocracy and power, since peasants had little chance of ever getting rich. To them, money was almost something imaginary, i.e. more mind than matter.

The feudal class connected to this suit is that of trade – the merchants and businessmen in the towns, who were increasingly successful through the centuries in actually getting rich. By the 19th century they even surpassed the wealth of the aristocracy.

Cups or Hearts

In present day texts on the Tarot, Cups is regarded as the third of the four suits. Its playing card counterpart Hearts, though, counts as the fourth and highest of the suits in many card games.

That may have to do with the corresponding Greek elements. Cups and Hearts resemble the principle of the element water, which is that of emotions. It's not the element usually placed first – although there was a Greek philosopher who stated firmly: *panta rei*, everything is floating.

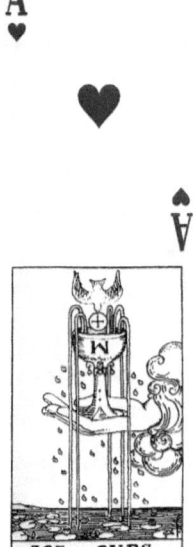

Since the playing cards have deviated from the symbolism and allegory of divination, they may have adapted the order these things mostly have in Christian thought.

Christian influence seems to have affected the playing cards more than the Tarot, since the latter has been more and more connected to a tradition of mysticism and magic, setting it apart from Christian dogma. The heart represents one feeling in particular, love, and none ranks higher in the values preached by Christianity. That's why this suit is connected to the feudal class of clergy. The church was one of the heart – or should be, at least.

The order between the suits in the Minor Arcana of the Tarot is of much less significance than the values assigned to the suits of the playing cards. So, what became necessary to decide with the playing card deck was more or less ignored with the Tarot.

In any case, the Cups and the Hearts are all about emotions and their influence, as is the element water.

Swords or Spades

The last of the four Tarot suits is that of Swords. Its counterpart in the regular playing card deck is Spades. Although most texts on the Tarot present it as the highest or at least the last of the four, in card games Spades is often second to Hearts.

As for the heightened value put on Hearts, I've given some thoughts above. When it comes to Swords being the last of the Minor Arcana in the Tarot, an evident explanation would be the sword's connection to aristocracy and power. But there's an additional ingredient, relating to the Greek element.

Swords and Spades are connected to the Greek element fire, which stands for activity and pure power. It's the element of the four that's always mentioned first, since it's linked to the vernal equinox, the 21st of March, which was

the start of the year in ancient calendars. It's also the moment when the sun enters the Zodiac sign Aries, the cardinal fire sign.

So, what's first in one order is last in another, but in both cases signifying its importance.

Some sources claim this suit to belong to the Greek element air, which may stem from comparing the sword to the principle of justice – like the sword held by Justitia. The principle of law is a thing of the mind, as is the element air.

But law is made by those in power, and power is definitely closer to the element fire. Traditionally, justice was in the hands of the mighty. It probably still is. So, the idea of it may be air, but the reality of it is fire. And the sword, like any weapon, is very much about reality.

Therefore, the last and sort of most prominent of the suits in the Tarot is that of Swords, relating to power, principle, and the way of the warrior.

In the Christian tradition, this type of virtue has been questioned and another has taken its place at the top: that of emotions, primarily love – the Hearts suit in the playing card deck. It doesn't matter much that the Tarot and playing cards differ at this point, since the Tarot rarely gives significance to any relative value between suits. They stand for different things, simply, in no particular order.

The only distinction in value made by the Tarot is between the Minor and the Major Arcana. But that's outside the comparison between Tarot and playing cards, since the latter have no such thing.

The pip cards of the Marseille Tarot deck's Pentacles (also called Coins).

Pip and Court

The Rider-Waite Tarot deck has illustrations for all the 78 cards, both the 22 of the Major Arcana and the 56 of the Minor Arcana. Playing cards, though, only have images for twelve of the 52 cards – the court cards. The remaining 40 pip cards, the Ace to ten of each suit, only have repetitious patterns of their suit symbols. This facilitated the making of them, when printing was much more of a hands-on craft.

Actually, most Tarot card decks through the centuries have been produced similarly to the playing cards, with rudimentary illustrations for the pip cards. In the beginning, all the Tarot cards were painstakingly hand-painted. They still had elaborate images, but not the pip cards.

That changed with the Rider-Waite deck. Most decks

The Pentacles (also called Coins) pip cards of the Etteilla Tarot. He started adding more imagery to each pip card than previous versions, but not to the extent of the Rider-Waite deck to follow a century later.

that followed also illustrated every card. But the simpler solution for the pip cards is still around in the type of deck called the Tarot of Marseille, as well as other designs.

Except for the delight of elaborate images on at least some of the cards, there was probably also a political necessity for making the court cards stand out. Dealing with kings and queens and such, everybody had to show proper respect and admiration. Colorful images to represent them were mandatory.

The court cards also imply that the link between the suits and the four feudal classes is not the dominant one. Peasants were not allowed to be kings, nor were merchants, whereas the kings of the clergy had other titles

The court cards of the Marseilles Tarot deck.

completely and nobody would dare to deviate from them. Kings came from the aristocracy, so that was the only class obviously and acceptably linked to royalty.

In the imaginations of past minds, the four suits might rather have given an impression of four kingdoms. If so, Cups (Hearts) would have been a sea-faring one, such as an island kingdom. Wands (Clubs) would be an inland realm, thriving on farming. Pentacles (Diamonds) would be a country of commerce, like the city states of Renaissance Italy, trading goods from far away to far away. Swords (Spades) would be a warring state, constantly battling to increase its territory.

The above is pure speculation, of course, but such thoughts wouldn't be alien to minds of our past. And it would explain why the pip cards were usually not illustrated. Except for the court, the population of a kingdom was not that important in any other way than its quantity.

Tarot
Spreads

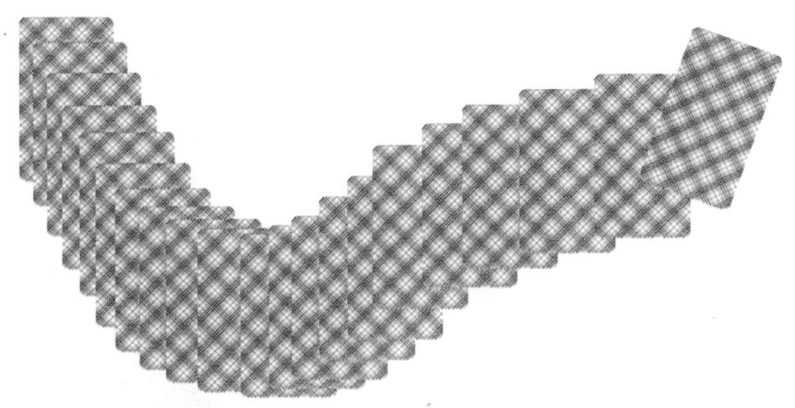

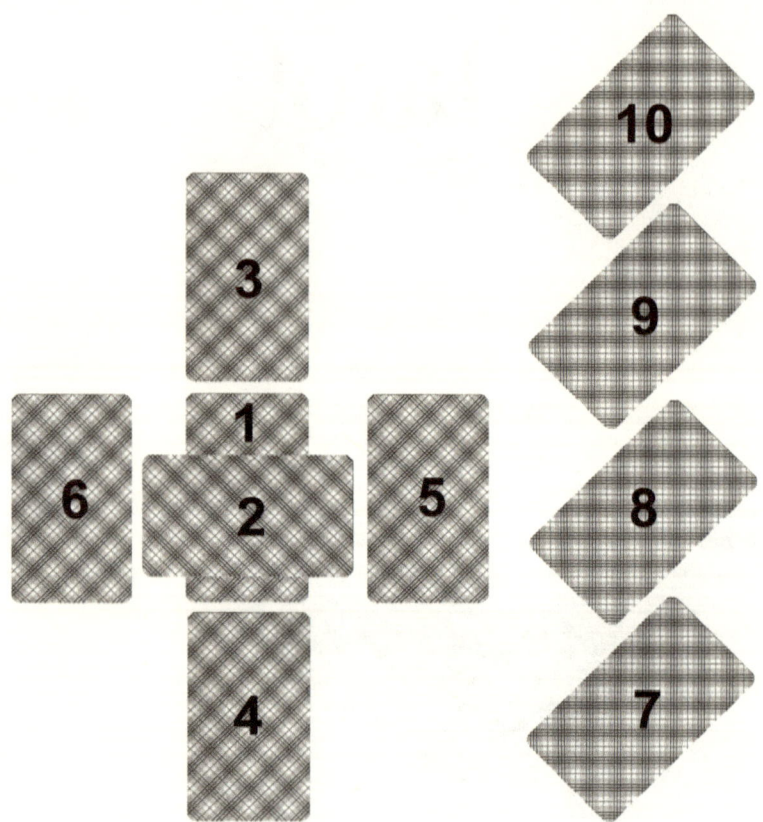

*The Celtic Cross, the most famous and used of the Tarot card
divination spreads. Here are the meanings of the ten cards:*

1 *Your condition at present.*
2 *Your obstacle and trouble at present.*
3 *The best possible outcome for you.*
4 *The cause to your present situation.*
5 *Your immediate past.*
6 *Your immediate future.*
7 *You at present.*
8 *Your surroundings at present.*
9 *Your hopes and fears.*
10 *The outcome.*

The Celtic Cross

There are many different spreads used for divination with the Tarot cards, but by far the most popular one is the Celtic Cross, with ten cards from the Tarot deck in the positions shown on the image.

It was included in A. E. Waite's instructions to the Tarot deck of his own design from 1909. He called the spread an ancient Celtic method, which is uncertain. It may be his own invention, or a modification of cross style spreads used earlier in Tarot divinations.

Outside the Tarot use, a Celtic cross is the term for a cross combined with a circle, like the one on the right, originat-  ing in Ireland in Medieval times.

There's no other spread even re- motely as established and popular, which makes it a good starting point for working with the Tarot. I recommend it, too. The Celtic Cross, with its ten cards representing the same number of perspectives, sheds plenty of light to any question.

I would say, though, that the Celtic Cross may not be the perfect spread to bring light to a specific question one might be pondering. It's more general, describing a person's complete situation in life at the time of the divi- nation. Instead of giving the answer to a very specific question, it points out what that question would be and the circumstances making it particularly relevant for the moment. It describes what you should be asking yourself, and lays out your present situation as a whole.

But that's precisely its forte, particularly valuable for someone starting out with the Tarot. It gives direction for how to proceed with using Tarot divination to reflect on one's life and events in it. The Celtic Cross is the preferable spread for getting familiar with the Tarot.

As for finding the answer to a specific question or the outcome of a certain situation, you may want to try a spread with fewer cards, like one of those presented later in this book.

How to do it

After the Tarot deck has been shuffled and cut a few times, place ten cards, faces down, in the assigned order (see the image at the beginning of the chapter), which is also the order in which to flip and read them. As for how to interpret each card, see the chapters on the Major and Minor Arcana later in this book.

It's important to make the spread with faces down, so that you concentrate on one card at a time when flipping it. This also makes it possible for you to explore the reading step by step, widening and deepening the perspective gradually.

It's also important that you don't start shuffling before you're clear about what you want the divination to concern. The more you're aware of what you search for, the likelier it is that you find it. As stated above, I recommend that you allow the Celtic Cross to describe your general state at present, at least the first time you do it. The more precise your request, the less appropriate this spread is for it.

Of course, a complex life choice situation is excellently treated by the Celtic Cross, if the direction you need to consider will have considerable effect on several aspects of your future. What it handles less well is something isolated to just a small part of your life. Think big and you'll find that the Celtic Cross does, too.

Here's what each card represents (in the literature on the Tarot, there are slight variations regarding the meanings described below, but not significantly so):

1 Your condition at present

If you had a specific question, this card shows your condition in relation to it, otherwise your general condition – more precisely what stands out in it and affects you the most.

Some Tarot guides instruct you to choose this card yourself. I don't recommend that, since you might presuppose things that dim the answers. If you decide what your present condition is by choosing the card to represent it, Tarot will be unable to correct you. We don't always know ourselves that well.

2 Your obstacle and trouble at present

The card represents obstacles in relation to your specific question, if you had one, otherwise what's most troublesome for you at the moment. You need to consider this card in relation to the previous one, which is why it's on top of it. The obstacles pointed out  are those troubling your condition at present. So, they can be both minor and momentary. The following cards will bring light to that.

3 The best possible outcome for you

This card shows a possible future, and not what's really going to happen. It points out the ideal outcome either in relation to your specific question, or generally concerning your present condition and obstacles. Where  you stand today and what you wrestle with right now may lead to what this card shows – if you're able to make it happen.

4 What caused your present situation

If you had a question, this card says what the root of that situation is. Otherwise it reveals what has caused your present condition as a whole. Together with the previous cards it forms a chain of events, following the prin- 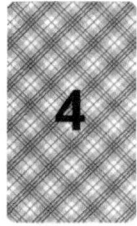 ciple of cause and effect. This card presents the cause, an event or condition influencing you at present. You wrestle with its effect. And the third card hint at what would be the outcome if nothing else influenced the situation. But there's always more in life.

5 Your immediate past

This depends on the time span the question suggests, or the time during which you've had your present condition and obstacles. The card shows what preceded your present situation – not necessarily having caused it, but somehow anyway leading up to it. That can be way back in the past or very recently. This card shows what the past looks like in light of the present situation.

6 Your immediate future

This is what to expect, no matter what you do. How far into the future depends on your question or the type of your present condition as well as the severity of its obstacles. It can also be to the moment of a significant event having just about nothing to do with your present situation, but still very important to you. The card completes a horizontal timeline from the past through the present to the near future – as things look right now. Every moment has its own timeline, so the past can change as quickly as the present, and the future reshapes accordingly.

This card is the last of the basic cross of this spread. You can stop here if you just want to make a time based divination, relating to a certain situation or problem. The following cards add perspectives of a wider kind, relating to your personality and your subjective perception of the situation.

7 You at present

This card indicates who you are in general and how you relate to the theme of the question, if you had a specific one. It shows your personality, especially aspects of it relevant to  the situation at hand. You can change if circumstances do. But here's where you are and what you're like right now.

8 Your surroundings at present

This shows family, friends, and the environment you're in, especially that which relates to your question. It also shows how people around you and circumstances surrounding you influence the situation. No man is an island. The card gives clues to what in your social life  might put you in your spot and limit your ability to get out of it, or for that matter where you can find help solving things.

9 Your hopes and fears

The hopes and fears described by this card may be regarding the question, if you had a specific one, or generally in your life at this time. Notice that what you fear and what you wish is somehow the same. You wish to escape your fears and you fear you don't get what you wish. But  profoundly, they are closely related, like the two sides of a coin. Be careful with what you wish for, since you may get it. Don't flee what you fear, before being sure that it will not benefit you in some way.

10 The outcome

This card shows the conclusion in regard to the question, if there was one, otherwise how this phase of your life ends up. It's usually hard to grasp this card's meaning, other than superficially. That's because a final outcome  is often distant and involves other events than those considered at present, many of them hard to imagine. The future has surprises in store for us all. No divination can protect us from that, because what we haven't experienced yet, we don't comprehend even if we get it predicted. So, regard this card as a clue, but don't expect to solve the riddle until you get there.

Things to Think About

When you try the Celtic Cross or any other Tarot card spread, it's important that you have a question in mind beforehand. Write it down before starting the Tarot spread, so that you have no doubts about what you really asked. It will help you tremendously in understanding the answer the Tarot gives.

If you don't have a question, the Tarot spread will tell you about your present situation in general and the significant things in its past and future. The Tarot will sort of choose what's important for you to consider at this point in your life. That's a good way of discovering the question you should have asked, if you would have been consciously aware of it. We don't always know ourselves that well, but we snap it when we get a glimpse of it.

As for the meaning of each card position in the Celtic Cross or any other spread, you do well to ponder it before trying the spread the first time – and again for each position before flipping the card and watching its image. If you do this properly, the card's image will give an immediate response that you grasp intuitively, which is always the best way.

My explanations of the meanings of the ten card positions above are not exactly the same as what you find in other books and websites about the Tarot. They all differ slightly. I've tried to make it as clear as possible, so that you have no doubt about the meaning of a card when you turn it.

You may prefer other definitions of the ten Celtic Cross positions, and that's fine. The important thing is that you're clear about it before you start a spread. Then you can invent your own system, and it will work fine for you. It works the better the more you are aware of the meaning you ascribe to each card position.

That's how it works. You decide, and then you do. If you're undecided, you'll have trouble understanding the result properly. When you're decided, it doesn't matter if that's far away from any common Tarot application. You'll make it work and it will have something valuable to tell you.

Therefore, don't worry much about rules on how to shuffle and how many times to cut the deck. That's just ritual. The important thing is that you are aware of what you're doing and how you intend to interpret the result. Tarot will adapt.

Reversed Cards

It's common to interpret a card differently if it's reversed – i.e. upside-down. I'm ambiguous about that, for several reasons.

It's common that practitioners of a system of divination make it overly complicated in an effort to make it say more. Usually, what it says to begin with is quite enough, if pondered properly. Having additional meanings depending on what way a card is facing doubles the information, but doesn't necessarily clarify it.

Regular playing cards are usually designed so that there's no upside-down. They look the same both ways. So, people who use such cards for divination make no difference depending on the angle of the card – since it's just not possible. With many Tarot cards it is evident what side is up or down, at least if they all have elaborate pictures. But that's far from all Tarot decks.

The Marseille Tarot deck from the 15th century, which is significantly older than the Rider-Waite one, has got many cards that look pretty much or completely the same reversed.

Some of the Rider-Waite Tarot cards become odd when reversed. The most obvious case is that of the Hanged man, who hangs upside-down on the card. Reversed he doesn't hang at all.

The Pentacles pip cards of the Marseille Tarot. Only the 7 and the 3 look significantly different upside-down.

The Hanged Man of the Rider-Waite Tarot, straight and reversed.

There are other complications with a special meaning for a reversed card. Usually, divination by Tarot is done by someone for another, who sits at the opposite side of the table. So, what's reversed for one is regular for the other. Confusion ensues.

My main objection, though, is that the opposite meaning of a card is already implied in the image and included in the assigned meaning to it. Simply put, any situation has a positive and a negative side to it, so there's always the possibility of both.

Even the dreaded card Death of the Major Arcana can mean putting an end to something and thereby breaking completely free of it. Death is the Reaper, but also in many cases a liberator. The Tower card indicates some kind of catastrophe, but as horrible as it sounds, that can be cleansing, opening up for a new solution by which everyone involved gains. And so on.

A. E. Waite, the author of the Rider-Waite Tarot card deck, instructed in different readings for cards in regular or reversed positions. It makes some sense on his deck, but I would still say that it should be considered carefully before being applied to the reading.

If you're comfortable with it, go right ahead – but otherwise, watch the images on the cards and let your intuition guide you to the meaning regarding the specific question and situation, and don't worry about the card's angle when you turn it.

That also spares you the trouble of figuring out how to flip the cards – from one of its sides or from the top or bottom.

Some of the most dreaded cards of the Tarot. They all have positive aspects as well.

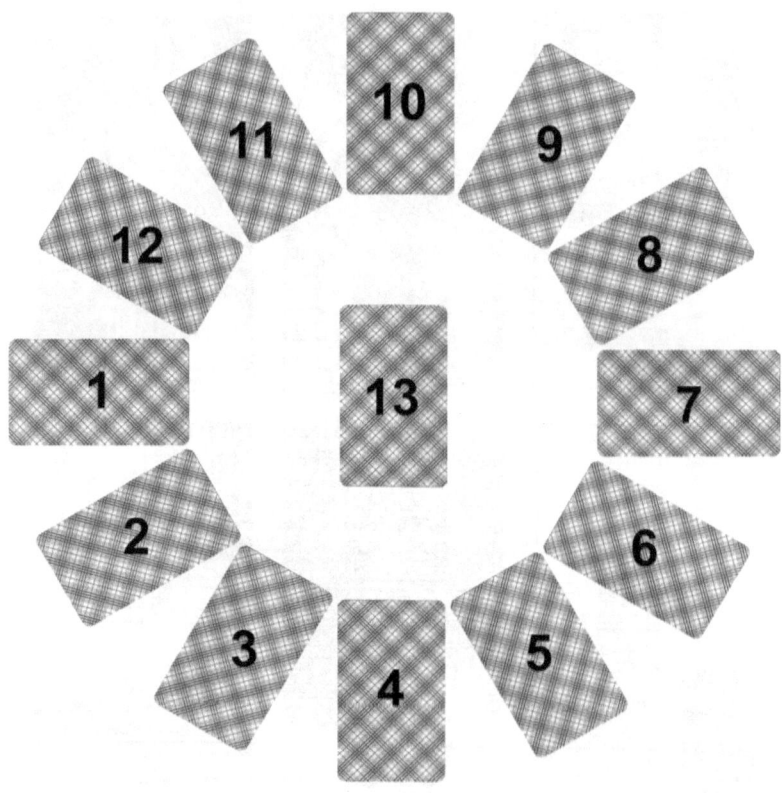

The Horoscope House Spread, based on the twelve astrological Houses of the horoscope chart. Here are the meanings of the
cards:

1	Identity	8	The Unknown
2	Resources	9	Travel
3	Communication	10	Career
4	Home	11	Ideals
5	Pastime	12	Shortcomings
6	Work	13	Where you are right now
7	Partners		

The Horoscope House Spread

A Tarot spread of similar complexity to that of the Celtic Cross is one based on the horoscope birth chart structure, which is excellent in particular to those who are familiar with astrology and its principles.

The horoscope chart is a circle divided into the twelve Zodiac signs, but it also contains a separate division into twelve astrological Houses, each representing a certain part of one's life. The latter works quite well also for a Tarot card spread.

Astrology is one of the most ancient methods of prediction and by far the most influential one through history in just about every culture. Its symbols are well-defined, intuitively familiar to each of us, much in line with what C. G. Jung called archetypes. Its system makes sense to the human mind without too much effort. So, through the perspective of astrology, it's possible to quickly reach a deep understanding of how to use and read the Tarot.

The Horoscope House Spread is simply a circle of twelve Tarot cards, each representing one of the twelve astrological Houses, its image revealing your situation in relation to what that House stands for.

You may also add a thirteenth card in the center of the circle, which is where the Earth is in the horoscope chart. That card represents your general situation, where and what you are right now. Since that would already be expressed by the sum of the other cards, you can also leave it out.

How to do it

Start by contemplating what it is you want to learn from doing the Tarot divination. For the Horoscope House Spread as well as for the Celtic Cross, described earlier, the best is really to avoid specific questions. This spread works the best when allowed to describe your complete situation, instead of you limiting it to one or other minor problem. This way you are also open to perspectives of which you may have been unaware.

Shuffle the cards, focused on the issue at hand, and make the spread, faces down, in the order given on the image at the beginning of this chapter – counterclockwise. It's the same order as that of the astrological Houses, starting at the left side, which represents the eastern horizon in the horoscope chart.

So, the first six cards are below the horizon and the next ones above it. That which is below the horizon represents the private sector of your life, such as family and friends. Above the horizon are the social aspects of your life. But that's just one way of looking at it. Consider instead the meaning of each House, which is of higher relevance.

The last card is the one in the middle, if you choose to add it. It's also the one to flip the last, by which you may find that it comes as no surprise considering what the previous twelve cards have shown.

Flip one card at a time, from the first to the twelfth House card, but make sure to contemplate what the House represents before doing so.

Here's what each House represents (there are slight differences in the literature on astrology about House meanings, but the below is quite well established):

1 Identity

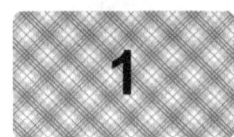

This House shows how others see you. It starts with how you present yourself, but when people get to know you better they start to see through that and gradually discover what they perceive as the real you. That's not necessarily any truer about your personality, but it's the impression you give.

2 Resources

This House rules your personal resources, which include your economy as well as your abilities. It's what you have at your disposal, almost always and in spite of what may happen. Your capacity as it is when depending on nothing other than yourself.

3 Communication

Here are your friends and acquaintances, the people you meet daily and regard as your closest entourage, so to speak, or prefer to hang out with. It's also the House of your basic education, what you've picked up while growing into an adult. Any higher education, though, is marked by the 9th House.

4 Home

This House shows your home and family, the private sector that you protect and regard as your own. It's actually the same House for the home you grew up in and the one you form for yourself and your own family. This is simply what home is like to you, and those who inhabit it together with you.

5 Pastime

This House shows your personal preferences, pleasures and interests, as you will have them when you're able to choose for yourself. It's what you do for your own sake. Many astrologers claim that it also shows your children and your relation to them, but I find that questionable – it depends on what you feel about them and if you like to spend your pastime with them.

6 Work

This is the House of your daily work – not the workplace as such, but what you do there and how you manage the things that are expected of you. So, it's your profes-

sion and not the company that hires you. The House describes what kind of work you do, and how it works out.

7 Partners

This is the House of your partners – those of love as well as in other types of relations. It shows the nature of your cooperation and commitment to another person. That's a pattern repeating itself from lover to lover, also somewhat the same in business relations, alliances formed, and so on. You tend to form any kind of couple sort of the same way, although your purposes and activities differ.

8 The Unknown

The things you cannot control are marked by this House. That includes your bloodline, since you have no way of choosing your relatives and what they bring. It also regards fate in the way it strikes unexpectedly, giving you no chance to escape it. Of course, sometimes it benefits you. The occult and matters beyond the palpable and controllable world are also here, especially your attitude to them.

9 Travel

This House deals with major and lasting changes to your life as a whole, and how you adapt to them. That's more than travel, but the traditional way in which great changes to one's life happened was often through travel – moving elsewhere, settling in a foreign place. Also, higher education belongs here, since it expands your horizon and pretty much decides what your professional life will be afterwards.

10 Career

This is the House of your social status, your significance in your social environment and how you handle it. It's the House of kings and other high leaders, but also of the respect you're given by others, whatever your title  and position may be. Your career definitely belongs to this House, also if you shun it. It's what you make of your life in the eyes of others.

11 Ideals

Your ideals and your interaction in the community are revealed by this House. Its major role is what you do for others, not for yourself, and there- fore also what impression you give them in this perspective. It's how you relate to people in groups so big you  can't know everybody's name and face. We are nothing without ideals, whatever they are, and this House shows the characteristics of yours, as well as how you live up to them.

12 Shortcomings

This House shows your sacrifices, what you are unable to express because of other things in life that take their tolls and restrain you. It's also the House of your dreams and fan-tasies, since they are by nature outside the so called real world. The more you have to sacrifice, the richer your dreams will be – and remain such. The House is called the Hell of the horoscope, but that's a simplification. What are we without our dreams? One life is not enough for all we'd like of it, so we have our dreams to fill it beyond its capacity. That hurts, but it can be a sweet pain.

13 Where you are right now

This card doesn't represent any House but sort of the sum of them. If you choose to use this card, it shows your general situation at the moment, where and what you are at this point in time. When you have properly con-sidered all the previous twelve Houses as the cards have described them, this card should come as no surprise.

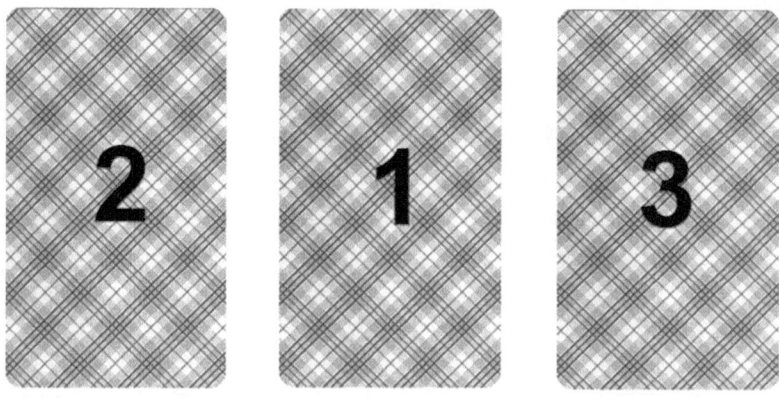

The Time Trio Spread, suitable for any kind of specific question or situation. Observe the order in which the cards should be read, indicated by their numbers. Here are the meanings of the cards:

1 *The present*
2 *The past*
3 *The future*

The Time Trio Spread

Now, a much easier spread than the previous ones. This one you can use any moment when a question pops up in your mind. It answers by the three tenses: past, present, and future. That's why I name it the Time Trio Spread. It reveals what your situation is now, what led up to it, and to what it will lead.

This is the core of what you want to know in most situations. If the problem is not too complicated, that's enough.

So, don't use this spread when pondering your life situation in general, or when trying to sort out existential stuff pertaining to your whole life. The result is too narrow to encompass the vast complexity of existence. But if you are bothered by some certain aspect, a specific problem, or a momentary complication – then you may find this spread rewarding, giving you a fresh perspective and some clues on how to act.

How to do it

Don't forget to think carefully about the question at hand, already when shuffling your cards. Write it down if you can. You don't want to be uncertain about the exact wording of your inquiry when it's time to interpret what the cards say.

It's very important that you follow the order given by the illustration, both when you make the spread and when you flip the cards, one at a time. That's because time is an illusion. Only the present exists, but it rests on the past and it pounces towards the future. Understanding your situation always starts by correctly perceiving the present. When you do that, you can examine the past leading up to it and the future coming as a result of it.

So, follow the order given, starting with the present. After contemplating what the card of the present reveals to you, it's time to dig into the past. That way you get clues as to what caused the present. Without having some kind of grasp of how the past led to the present, you have no clue as to how you can influence the process from the present to the future.

If you ask the Tarot or any other method of divination about the future, it means you hope to influence it somewhat – by preparing for it or maybe even changing it slightly. That can't be done without some knowledge of how the past led to the present. I can't stress this enough. It's at the core of the paradigm of divination. Without this understanding, you get nowhere.

When you've contemplated the card of the past properly and seen its link to the card of the present, then it's time to look at the card of the future. If it doesn't reveal a chain of events making sense through the three cards, you are probably unable to penetrate the mystery of the situation you're in. If so, try it again later, when you've experienced a little more and have an increased chance of seeing through the mist.

If you apply this simple spread correctly, it can be a great asset. And there's no problem too small to try it on. Using it frequently, you learn about how Tarot can be of use to you, so don't hesitate.

Just don't make the spread about the same situation or question repeatedly. That will backfire. Tarot, like most methods of divination, has a built-in lack of patience.

Here's what each card represents in the Time Trio Spread:

1   The Present

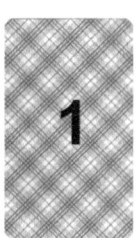

This card shows what the present situation is, regarding the specific problem or question you had in mind. It's not a general description of your present, but one focusing on the question at hand and the state of it at this very moment.

2   The Past

This card tells you what the past was like, in regard to your question. That can be a distant past, if your situation commenced long ago. Or it can be quite recent, if this is something new to you. The card describes the start and the cause, if there is one extractable. It may be difficult to interpret the card's meaning, but compare it to the card of the present and you should be able to see a link of some kind. That's the clue to understanding both your present situation and past events leading up to it.

3   The Future

Note that this card shows the future in rela-
tion to your question or problem, not neces-
sarily your future as a whole – or even the
most significant components of your future.
The card relates to what you ask and not to
what you may later find more important. In
some cases it actually does the latter, if that's alarming or
sensational enough, but don't bet on it. When you ask a
specific question you get an equally specific answer. And
when contemplating this third card, don't forget to compare it to the previous ones. You understand the answer
the Tarot gives, only to the extent you see the relation between the three cards of the spread – the chain of events
from the past through the present to the future.

The Yin Yang Spread

Here's a two card spread technique with a lot of applications. Basically it works on contradistinctions: either or, good and bad, positive and negative, constructive and destructive, and so on. You can surely find your own polarities, which make the most sense to you in divination.

Yin and yang are the Chinese opposites that ancient Chinese tradition regards as the dynamics behind the creation of the world, as well as its continued workings. Originally they meant the sunny and shady side, like those of a tree, but they expanded into a cosmos of opposites: male and female, heaven and earth, hot and cold, light and dark, and thousands of others. The same kind of cosmology can be found in many other cultures and societies. Indeed, there are reasons for it. The universe seems to be made up of opposites.

I think that the most rewarding way to use this simple spread is for finding the pros and cons of a choice you consider. So, use the spread for very specific questions in very specific situations. Otherwise the cards will be unable to give you any advice clear enough to utilize.

Life is full of such choices, so you'll have lots of opportunities to try the Tarot out on them.

In short, the spread is aimed at reflecting on an opportunity of any kind. An opportunity appears and you have

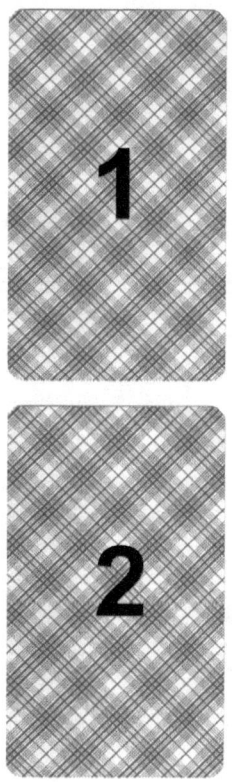

*The Yin Yang Spread, with which you can choose opposites for
your Tarot reading. In the case of a "pros" and "cons" reading,
here are the meanings of the cards:*
1   Pros
2   Cons

Tarot

to choose whether to go for it or not. You need to reflect the pros and cons.

There's no third card, so the Tarot isn't able to give its conclusion. It's because in this case, when you use this spread, you want to make the decision yourself. You just need to reflect on the matter in the very particular perspective the Tarot can give you. But the choice is yours. If that's not your cup of tea, try another of the Tarot spreads.

When the spread is used in the way I suggest above, it should really be called the Pro and Con Spread. But you may have other uses for it, so I kept the general name for this chapter.

How to do it

Of course, you could just lay the cards beside one another, but that doesn't point out their polarity clearly. You need to make their respective meaning evident, so you should find a method by which to enhance it.

I suggest putting one card above the other as seen on the picture, making the "pro" card the top and the "con" the bottom. That's usually how we relate to the good and bad – the former is above and the latter below, like heaven and hell. So, if you want to be intuitively aware of what each card represents, that might be a convenient solution in all its humbleness.

But which card to start with? It's important that you decide this beforehand, so as not to be confused about what the cards really represent. Do you want to see pro before con, the good news or the bad news first? If we don't press ourselves by trying to be patient, I think we're all most eager to see the pro card.

Why not? An opportunity is a thing of hope. We do well to long for it. Also, it usually encompasses some change in life, and change is good, or life just rushes by in a blur of identical days.

So, go for the pro card and explore it well, before examining the price involved. Everything has a price. That can't be escaped. Therefore, it's advantageous to start by considering how much you want what you're bound to pay for. Frequently in life, it's a good deal.

Here are the meanings of the cards, if you don't feel like altering them:

1 Pros
This card shows the benefits of the opportunity that has presented itself, all the good things that will come out of it. There's no time limit to this card's message. It is valid as long as the opportunity in question is not altered or ended. If you decide not to go for the opportunity, the card is not valid. What it suggests will not happen.

2 Cons
This card shows the bad effects of the opportunity, should you choose it. What's described is only the negative consequences of the opportunity and what it brings, not other aspects of your life. And like with the previous card, it's only valid if you grab the opportunity. If you don't, what the card shows is no longer valid.

Single Card Flip

The most easy and direct way to use the Tarot is by having one single card answer the question you ask yourself. That's suitable for simple questions relating to one clear problem or situation. It doesn't have to be the type of question that demands a yes or no answer, but not far from it. If your question is too complex, one card is hardly enough to answer it.

But there are lots of questions suitable for the one card Tarot inquiry. Once you've started, it's tempting to just go and go, as new questions pop up in your mind.

That can be fun for a while, but don't get swept away so that your questions get increasingly meaningless or banal, and don't come with them in a tempo that makes it impossible for you to contemplate each card's answer properly. Every divination method should be treated with sincerity and respect, or it quickly stops working for you.

As long as you have that in mind, you'll be fine.

How to do it

Here it's of utmost importance that you're really clear about what question you ask. You do well to write it down, or at least speak it out loud, so that you're certain about it. Don't shuffle your cards before you've done so.

Yes, you should shuffle the deck. Otherwise it's

meaningless. If you have several questions, you have to shuffle several times. If you don't, it just gets silly quite quickly. For example, the Tarot must be able to reveal the same card also for a later question, if that's the case.

How you pick the card is up to you, but the best is to spread the deck out – at least somewhat – and then pick a card, sort of like magicians want you to do when they do one of their tricks.

You can flip it immediately, since there are no other card positions to distract you. That's why I call this method the Single Card Flip. You just pick the card and flip it. Wam bam.

In the case of the Single Card Flip you can also choose to use just the Major Arcana, the 22 trump cards of the Tarot. Thereby, you can't expect very nuanced answers, but on the other hand they are clearer. The answer is a shout instead of a whisper.

I still wouldn't recommend you to do that, since it fosters a sort of melodramatic view on life. Everything isn't spectacular, but can still be interesting and rewarding. So, if you're not too intrigued by the noise of the Major Arcana, stick to using the whole Tarot deck.

When you flip the card, stay with it for a while, although it might be tempting to move on to other questions. The more you contemplate the image of that card, the more it can reveal about the question you asked – even things that were the farthest from your mind.

One single card can say a lot more than just yes or no. Actually, the Tarot cards are not very good at yes and no, but excellent at all the other stuff.

Tarot
Cards

THE FOOL.	THE MAGICIAN.	THE HIGH PRIESTESS	THE EMPRESS.	THE EMPEROR.
THE HIEROPHANT	THE LOVERS.	THE CHARIOT.	STRENGTH.	THE HERMIT.
WHEEL of FORTUNE.	JUSTICE.	THE HANGED MAN.	DEATH.	TEMPERANCE.
THE DEVIL.	THE TOWER.	THE STAR.	THE MOON.	THE SUN.

JUDGEMENT.

THE WORLD.

The Major Arcana

The Tarot card deck consists of two parts – the Major Arcana (also called the Trumps) with 22 cards and the Minor Arcana with the remaining 56 cards in four suits of 14 cards each.

The Major Arcana is unsuited. Its 22 cards don't belong to any of the four suits of the Tarot: Wands, Pentacles, Cups, and Swords. Instead, each Major Arcana card represents its own dignity – a character of significance, a mythical component, or an event of great importance.

As commented above, they can be compared to archetypes and should be seen as such. When you get a Major Arcana card in your Tarot spread, it signifies a particularly important event or circumstance regarding the question your spread is to answer.

In addition to my own comments, I've added the comprised description A. E. Waite made for each card. They don't always match mine completely. Furthermore, they deal with reversed cards, something I've chosen not to, as explained earlier in this book.

Waite also wrote more extensive comments on the Major Arcana cards, but they are filled with the occult symbols of his time and therefore rather difficult to relate to in the present.

THE MAGICIAN.

1   The Magician

A sudden solution, as if by magic
– but it may be just an illusion.

Among devoted Tarot users, the Magician is often the favorite card. That's because already using the Tarot is a kind of magic – opening the door to a reality yet to be explained in scientific terms, if that's ever going to be possible. The Magician seems to have everything in control, like a master of fate, but that might just as well be an illusion.

In our days, most magicians are illusionists, but the one of this card is the first to fall for the illusion. That's particularly true for those who favor this card. They want the illusion.

In the picture, the Magician has gathered the symbols of all four suits on his table, as if everything in the world is at his disposal. Hardly. If he believes it, he's more of a fool than the card with that name – because the real Fool knows he's a fool. That makes all the difference in the world, and it's precisely the weakness of the Magician.

The card indicates things being solved as if by magic. It can be a person making big problems disappear or splendid solutions appear as if out of nowhere. But life doesn't work like that. If it's too good to be true, it probably isn't.

Merlin, the archetype of magicians, appeared in legends during the Middle Ages. Illustration from the early 13th century book Merlin, by Robert de Boron.

The Magician's solutions will by time prove to be somewhat lacking. Either they don't last or they don't solve everything, so new problems will emerge – this time more difficult to handle.

That's not necessarily a bad thing, since the initial solution was probably urgent and beneficial. Without it, who knows what would have happened? It's just important to understand that the Magician's solution is rarely the final one. The problem is not really dealt with, but just made to disappear for a while. Still, that can be a blessing.

The Magician's weakness is to be overly confident. Just look at the sign for eternity like a halo above his head. So, we tend to be overly confident about solutions of that kind. When the card appears in your reading, expect a fantastic turn of events, but also watch out for what remains to be done – that which is at first invisible in the dazzle.

But who doesn't want to be dazzled, now and then?

A. E. Waite's description
Skill, diplomacy, address, subtlety; sickness, pain, loss, disaster, snares of enemies; self-confidence, will; the Querent, if male. Reversed: Physician, Magus, mental disease, disgrace, disquiet.

THE HIGH PRIESTESS

2   The High Priestess

Secrets and hidden circumstances
stand in the way and need to be understood.

The High Priestess is the ruler of what's hidden and secret, what lurks behind the scenes. She knows what really goes on. She's not that eager to reveal it, though, at least not to those who are fooled by the superficial. You have to deserve the revelations to which she holds the keys.

This card has a counterpart in that of the Hierophant, the pompous pope who is indeed powerful, but mainly carries the treasured symbols, having less to do with actual rulership. The High Priestess is the opposite – much more modest in appearance and rare in making public appearances, but still running the show.

She can be compared to a grey eminence, someone in charge although not carrying the office.

The High Priestess guards the secrets and ensures the master plan. In doing so, she knows to act with caution, very discreetly, and paying attention to details that are believed to be insignificant.

But it's in the shadows and the periphery that the future of the world is forged. The microcosm rules the macrocosm. The High Priestess is a master of the microcosm.

The original Grey Eminence: François Leclerc du Tremblay, right-hand man of Cardinal Richelieu in 17th century France. The ruler's advisor in the shadows is a recurring theme, in myth as well as in reality. Painting by Jean-Léon Gérôme, 1873.

When the card represents a person, it's someone who has the key to the solution, but holds on to it unless you are deemed worthy – and your intentions are the ones approved.

If the card refers to an event, there's a complicated problem needing to be solved, almost like a riddle, and you need to contemplate to see it. Others may not even realize that there's an obstacle, but if not recognized and dealt with, failure is certain – although it may come as a complete surprise and nobody knows why.

A. E. Waite's description

Secrets, mystery, the future as yet unrevealed; the woman who interests the Querent, if male; the Querent herself, if female; silence, tenacity; mystery, wisdom, science. Reversed: Passion, moral or physical ardor, conceit, surface knowledge.

3   The Empress

The gentle power that still rules,
almost unnoticed and rarely opposed.

The Empress is a ruler, make no mistake about that, but a gentle one getting her will by peaceful means. She suggests and convinces, making her choices seem like the only reasonable ones. Quite often they are. If you follow her you will have a pleasant ride, but if you oppose her it will all be uphill.

While the Emperor is armed for battle and eager to engage in it, the Empress remains on her throne, relaxed, getting things done seemingly without any effort. If the Emperor is a warrior, she's a politician. He might win the war, but she controls the land during the peace that follows.

Her ways are so soft and gentle that even her enemies feel blessed, while she strips them of their power and turns them into loyal subjects, whether they are aware of it or not.

She's what's called the enlightened monarch, an expression used (and debated) for rulers, especially of the late 18th century, who had cultural and academic ambitions for their countries inspired by the ideas of the Enlightenment.

Catherine the Great of Russia. One of the so-called enlight-ened monarchs, allegedly using wisdom instead of brute force to rule. Painting by Alexander Roslin, 1777.

One such monarch was Catherine the Great of Russia, on the painting by Alexander Roslin in 1777. There have been many others through history.

If the Tarot card represents a person, it's somebody very resourceful that you do best to humor and get on your side, or listen carefully to if that's not going to happen.

If it represents an event, it calls for calmness and carefully considered choices of action, since things are much more delicate than they may seem. Also, it suggests that if you find the patterns behind the obvious, then you can accomplish much more than anyone at first imagined.

A. E. Waite's description

Fruitfulness, action, initiative, length of days; the unknown, clandestine; also difficulty, doubt, ignorance. Reversed: Light, truth, the unraveling of involved matters, public rejoicings; according to another reading, vacillation.

THE EMPEROR.

4   The Emperor

You're up against real power,
so yield or suffer the consequences.

The Emperor has real concrete power in abundance. This is no politician in need of allies and careful diplomacy. He's raw force. Anybody dealing with him should yield or else perish. On the image, he sits firmly on the throne, but in armor – he will stand up and strike at the moment he is challenged. He tolerates nothing but obedience.

We've had a number of emperors through history, several of them so majestic that 'majesty' is not enough to describe them. One of the first and probably still the most impressive one was Alexander in the 4th century BC, who conquered most of the known world at that time, when he was still a young man.

Below is a later painting of the legendary moment when he cut the Gordian Knot, so complicated that the one to untie it was fit to rule the world. Alexander did so by swinging his sword – a warrior's solution.

The Emperor on this card is indeed a warrior ruler. He sits on a stone throne with his armor on, eager to do battle. The image on the card suggests another warrior ruler, the legendary King Arthur, but it might as well be Alexander, Julius Caesar, Napoleon, or Genghis Khan.

Alexander cuts the Gordian Knot, by Jean-Simon Berthélemy, 18th century. Alexander, who lived in the 4th century BC, is still regarded as one of the foremost conquerors.

It's the ruler with the force and the firmness to strike down any opposition.

So, if the Tarot card refers to a person, it's someone you just have to obey whether you want to or not. He or she has the power to decide the outcome and it would cost you very dearly indeed to oppose.

If the card refers to an event, you have to accept that the outcome is out of your hands. It's decided elsewhere and you just have to comply or suffer the consequences.

If the card is about you, though, it says that you have the power to force the outcome of your choosing, but probably not without a fight.

A. E. Waite's description

Stability, power, protection, realization; a great person; aid, reason, conviction; also authority and will. Reversed: Benevolence, compassion, credit; also confusion to enemies, obstruction, immaturity.

THE HIEROPHANT

5   The Hierophant

The dependency on approval
from an elevated dignity.

There's no doubt that the elevated figure on this Tarot card is the pope. The word hierophant is Greek, meaning someone who shows the holy. The card is sometimes called The High Priest, which is just about the same: the one claiming to be closest to what's holy, thereby kind of holy himself, too. But that's far from certain.

The pope and other kinds of high priests are heads of something symbolic, which is not the same as calling them symbolic heads. Usually, they have tremendous power and final say when it comes to what the deities may want. So, the deities seem mostly to want precisely what the hierophants want.

Temples are lavishly decorated, since they are to be the domains of gods. For the same reason, hierophants are lavishly dressed. Their appearances represent the splendor of what's holy, since they are supposed to be the closest links to it. That's why they can carry all that gold and jewels, without embarrassment. Some seem to indulge in it more than others, though.

In the Tarot deck, the Hierophant card is one that signals tremendous significance, but not necessarily as much

Pope Gregorius I. Painting by Francisco de Zurbaran, 1627.

Tarot

substance. Whatever the hierophant might claim, we're all just as bewildered before god. The divine has no definite location, so there's no way anybody could be nearer to it than others.

The high priest is head of rituals, but the essence of any spiritual path is what each of us makes of it inside ourselves. That's a temple no high priest can make his abode.

So, if the card refers to a person, it's someone very pompous indeed, whom it's of vital importance to treat with respect – whatever you might feel about it. You need that person's approval. At least, you can't afford offending him or her.

If the card refers to an event, it's a moment of great symbolic significance, which can lead to triumph or to debasement. There's not much more to do than hope for the best – and make sure not to offend anyone.

Watch out, because the Hierophant is a person or an event that is much more important to the final outcome than you might expect – definitely more than what seems reasonable.

A. E. Waite's description
Marriage, alliance, captivity, servitude; by another account, mercy and goodness; inspiration; the man to whom the Querent has recourse. Reversed: Society, good understanding, concord, over-kindness, weakness.

THE LOVERS.

6   The Lovers

Deeply felt mutual attraction
– for as long as it lasts.

Except for the nudity, the picture of the Lovers is quite innocent, maybe even virginal. That's because of the time and culture in which the deck of cards was created. Still, the card is definitely about sex, too. The complete love between two people. Attraction, lust, passion – all the emotions making two persons longing to connect, and then the devotion keeping them together for as long as it lasts.

The card is almost parodic in its emphasized innocence. The two lovers are not even holding hands, but remaining apart, forcefully separated by an angelic figure – albeit with red instead of white wings, as a discreet indicator of passion. The card speaks more of Agape than of Eros, the non-carnal love instead of the lustful one. No sin committed – yet.

Talking about sin, another one than that of the flesh is implied by the apple tree and the serpent on the left side. This certainly refers to Adam and Eve, and the forbidden fruit of the Tree of Knowledge. We know how that ended.

Innocence doesn't last for long, when love is involved. In a reading, this card is definitely about what its title says,

Adam and Eve in the Garden of Eden before the Fall, show-
ing some similarity to the Tarot card of the Lovers. Painting by
Masolino da Panicale, 1425.

and all the aspects thereof. Also, it's about the ability to love. It goes further. The card indicates a character in which love overshadows everything else. It's the card of the lover, whether it's a Casanova, a Cleopatra, or Tristan and Isolde. Those who live to love and love to live.

Falling in love depends on the ability to do so. The true lover is always in love, although the object may vary – still with complete fidelity to the love at the moment, as if suddenly nobody else exists in the whole world, and nothing else matters.

The lovers on this card seem innocent, actually not in love at all. But that's just because their eyes haven't even met yet. The man has spotted the woman and as soon as her eyes leave the angelic figure towering over their heads, she will see him and their nature will do the rest. They have it in them, so they're destined to fall in love if they just meet.

Therefore, the angel seemingly keeping them apart is one of opportunity, arranging fate so that it makes them meet. Not a difficult task with two lovers at heart. It can happen with just about anyone they meet, and certainly when both are of the same nature, like the ones on this card. Whether it was the angel's doing or not that they met, once it happened the heavenly creature would not be able to tear them apart.

A. E. Waite's description
Attraction, love, beauty, trials overcome. Reversed: Failure, foolish designs. Another account speaks of marriage frustrated and contrarieties of all kinds.

7   The Chariot

Triumph
– but beware of its consequences at length.

This Tarot card is about triumph in worldly matters. Like Caesar returning from a successful campaign, receiving the cheers of the Romans. A moment of greatness, but also a risk of megalomania. Success can destroy character quicker than adversity builds it.

The Roman emperors used to have a slave with them on the triumphal chariot, whispering repeatedly in their ear: "Remember that you're only human." It was to help them stay grounded through all the praise.

Julius Caesar ended that tradition. It didn't do him any good.

On the next page is a painting of Julius Caesar on his chariot, made by Andrea Mantegna in 1492.

Triumph is indeed cause for concern. There are two main risks with it: one's own state of mind and the reversing feelings of the people. When you are adored you quickly lose perspective and see yourself as larger than life in any mirror. People who loved you in your moment of triumph will love to despise you as soon as they see you fail.

So, at the moment of success – beware!

A triumphant and grim faced Julius Caesar on his chariot. Painting by Andrea Mantegna in 1492.

If the Tarot card relates to a person, it's someone who grants success with whatever is at hand – also yours, even if your accomplishment might not have been decisive.

If it relates to an event, it indicates a most fortunate outcome, but you have to consider what the long-term consequences might be, envy from others definitely being one of them.

The trick to accomplish lasting success is to be modest about it, and that's not always easy.

A. E. Waite's description

Succor, providence, also war, triumph, presumption, vengeance, trouble. Reversed: Riot, quarrel, dispute, litigation, defeat.

8   Strength

Strength of a kind that's superior
because of its clever application.

The strength on the picture of this card seems delicate: a maiden pure at heart holds the jaws of a lion, rendering it harmless. That's real strength, far beyond what mere muscles can accomplish. It's so powerful because it has an ideal.

It's very significant that she masters the lion not by forcing its jaws apart, like any Tarzan would, but by pressing them together. That, too, stops it from biting. The lion has become harmless and its tongue suggests that it enjoys this. So, it's the strength of neutralizing strength. A beneficial paradox.

Some would say that the Tarot card is not about strength at all, but the path away from it. Maybe so. But strength is a force that tends to yield only to superior strength. Therefore, it can only be pacified by being defeated. That's the fundamental weakness of strength and the strength of weakness. What yields will prevail, what resists will break, *Tao Te Ching* has told us.

An expressive example of this is Achilles, the hero of great strength who had just one weakness: his heel. That's where his mother held him when dipping the infant

Achilles, just as the fatal arrow strikes his heel, the great hero's only weakness. Roman sculpture.

Achilles in the potion that made the rest of his body invulnerable. This tiny weakness killed him. Every strength has one.

The lion has mighty muscles by which to close its jaws on a prey, but not nearly as much strength to open them. Evolution slipped on that detail. Real strength is to utilize such weaknesses. That way, little strength is needed and still not even the strongest in the world can resist.

If this card refers to a person, it's someone who knows how to apply the resources to where they accomplish the most. Such strength is power.

If the card refers to an event, it would be one where victory went where it seemed the least likely. Strength, as most things human, is in the mind.

A. E. Waite's description
Power, energy, action, courage, magnanimity; also complete success and honors. Reversed: Despotism, abuse of power, weakness, discord, sometimes even disgrace.

THE HERMIT.

9   The Hermit

The lesson and reward,
but also misfortune,
of solitude.

The picture of the Hermit is a gloomy one. That's because of the solitude the card represents. Although voluntary in the case of a hermit, solitude is still somewhat sad. It's not chosen as a wish of separating oneself from fellow human beings, but for a certain purpose where being alone is instrumental. Usually, it involves an effort to get to know oneself at depth. That's why the Hermit is often linked to wisdom. That can be discussed.

The Hermit might find out plenty about himself and what goes on in his own mind, when avoiding the company of others. But that's in his mind, the ultimately secluded place where no one else can go. It rarely applies to the outside world, so the scope of any wisdom reached is limited, indeed. You go inwards to learn about yourself, but you have to go outside to learn anything about the world and your place in it.

The lantern in his hand and the dim blue background suggest night. The stillness and closed eyes of the Hermit suggest repose, even sleep. The self-discovery one does on one's own is like a dream, fading away quickly when one opens one's eyes.

Saint Paul the Hermit. Paul of Thebes was the first Christian hermit, according to the legend living between c. 228 and c. 341, which would make him 113 years old at death, being a hermit for 90 of them. Painting by Jusepe de Ribera, 17th century.

It's said that we're always alone at heart, in our souls. That's true in a sense, but it's also true that we never are. We have so much in common that wherever we go, even inside our minds, others have done the same and discovered the same. We are alike.

Therefore, the experience of one person, no matter how internal, has some relevance to all others. In that way, the Hermit can become wise.

But the wisdom reached has no substance before it's shared. What we discover in our loneliness becomes real when we share it with others and thereby discover that there's so much we share. In this manner, loneliness can be the way out of the loneliness.

It's not sure that this Hermit will come to that revelation. He seems committed to stay on his own, as if renouncing the world altogether. That leads nowhere. He must snap out of it, lift his head and open his eyes. Until then, he's in sort of a coma.

Still, occasionally in life we all need a recluse. To contemplate what we have been through and what we can expect in the future, to heal from emotional wounds, or simply to get some rest. It's a healing process, but it's not a final destination.

A. E. Waite's description
Prudence, circumspection; also and especially treason, dissimulation, roguery, corruption. Reversed: Concealment, disguise, policy, fear, unreasoned caution.

WHEEL of FORTUNE.

10 The Wheel of Fortune

An uncertain outcome,
with an aftermath to be carefully considered.

The Wheel of Fortune looks like a roulette. The outcome is uncertain, no matter what you do, so you can only hope to be lucky. The one thing to be expected is surprise. Sometimes fate plays tricks on us, and what can we do but wish for the best? You need to look beyond this point of time to get a glimpse of how the outcome will affect you – winning the lottery or losing a costly bet. If you worry, maybe you just shouldn't take this path.

The powerful methods of divination (that's most of them) have no problem revealing the future. But sometimes it's like they just don't want to, as if that's against some master plan concealed from us. This card of the Tarot deck is a reminder of this, whenever it appears in a reading. Don't try to know everything in advance. It's not allowed.

At heart we have to agree with it. What's the fun of living if there are no uncertainties and no surprises? We thrive on curiosity. Like any nutrition, it only keeps working if we keep feeding on it. What's hidden from us, even in divination, mainly has this function – keeping us awake and eager to meet tomorrow.

The Wheel of Fortune. Illustration attributed to Albrecht Dürer, from the book Ship of Fools by Sebastian Brant, 1494. The concept existed already in Ancient Greece and Rome. According to the Roman myth, the goddess Fortuna was at the wheel.

No doubt, the most evident modern version of the Wheel of Fortune is the roulette. The game as we know it was introduced in Paris, 1796.

As a personal characteristic, the Wheel of Fortune card indicates too much trust in chance. Happy-go-lucky. Some people are blessed with a multitude of joyous tidings, so it may work for them – mostly. Never always. Even the luckiest among us will be struck by misfortune, now and then. If they trusted luck too much, such a blow can be devastating to them and they may find that they lack any kind of insurance, any alternative by which to minimize the losses.

So, the Wheel of Fortune can signal a formidable opportunity ahead, but always also a warning: Don't bet your whole fortune on the most fortunate outcome. Save something for a rainy day. Consider in advance what you can do if things don't go your way.

A. E. Waite's description

Destiny, fortune, success, elevation, luck, felicity. Reversed: Increase, abundance, superfluity.

JUSTICE .

11 Justice

Justice without blindfold
is not always fair.

The Justice of the Tarot is not blind. There's the sword representing the sharp firmness of the law, and the scales by which to judge the actions of men, as carried by every image of Justitia. But no blindfold, the guarantee that all people are treated as equals before the law. Unfortunately, that has often proven not to be the case.

The blindfold on the personification of justice appeared at the end of the 15th century, as on the 1543 statue by Hans Gieng below, which may be the first known representation of blindfolded justice.

By excluding the blindfold, the Tarot card indicates that the system of justice is hazardous even to the innocent. You need not only to obey the law, but give the impression of doing so. That's not always easy. How can you prove that you are a law-abiding citizen? A basic principle of justice is that we are innocent until proven guilty, but in reality it has happened far too often through history that we've been regarded as guilty until we were able to prove our innocence – beyond any reasonable doubt.

This Tarot card, then, refers to the judgmental attitude – the one expecting and seeing faults in others and not in

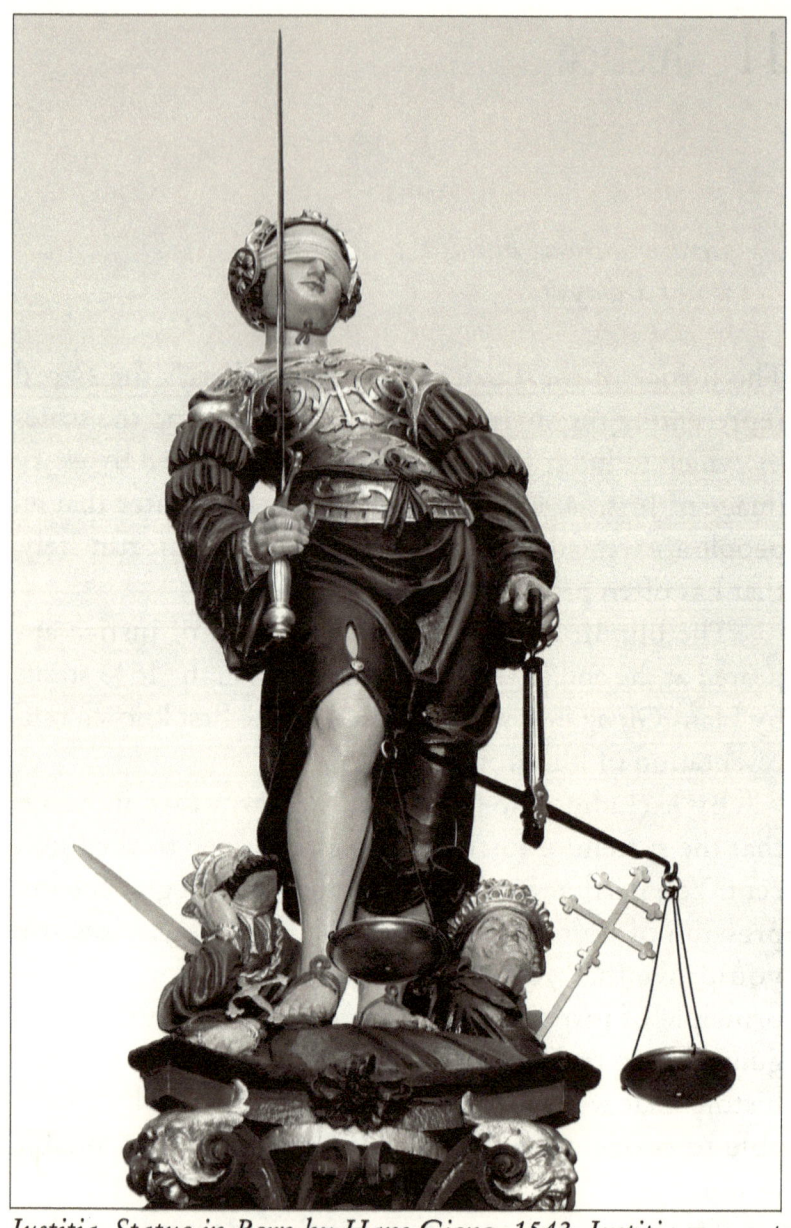

Justitia. Statue in Bern by Hans Gieng, 1543. Justitia was not blindfolded until at the end of the 15th century.

a hurry to reconsider or forgive. But if you stand the test you are acquitted, most definitely, and everything will be fine. You may even receive respect.

Notice also that the sword is held high, as if to strike, whereas the scales are held low. That's an indication of values between them in the mind of this figure of justice: Fairness in trial is of less importance than the order imposed by the might of the law. So, beware of Justice in this shape.

Even if you come out of it free of any accusations, you can't be sure that it's because of justice being done or just because you pleased the court. That's a victory with a bitter taste to it and a remaining sense of uncertainty.

The other great uncertainty with justice is the elusive nature of truth. As Pilate asked rhetorically: What is truth? We are rarely sure of having found it, extremely rarely all of it and nothing but it. So, who can judge, really?

Still, Justice on the picture of this card shows no hint of humility or hesitation. Not much benefit of a doubt is to be expected. A person with this characteristic needs to learn moderation and consideration. We all err. That goes for judges, too.

Compare the other Tarot card about justice: Judgment.

A. E. Waite's description
Equity, rightness, probity, executive; triumph of the deserving side in law. Reversed: Law in all its departments, legal complications, bigotry, bias, excessive severity.

XII

THE HANGED MAN.

12   The Hanged Man

Great personal sacrifice
that still doesn't hurt much.

The Hanged Man is about personal sacrifice, of course.
But this figure seems not to be broken, although hanging
upside-down. He will bounce right back, as soon as he
manages to get free. It's not that he heals easily. He is one
of the few who are not hurt to begin with, as if invulnerable. Maybe that's what tempts other people to use him as
a scapegoat.

He has a halo, and not a small one at that. Hanging
from the wooden structure, it makes him look a bit like
Jesus on the cross. The martyr. He's probably hanging
upside-down not to bear too much resemblance with
Christ, which would have been blasphemy in the time
when this image took its shape.

There's a parallel to this in the early history of the
Christians. The disciple Peter was crucified and asked to
be done so upside-down, according to some old sources,
because he felt unworthy of the same death as his master.

But the Hanged Man is a martyr that neither dies nor
suffers that tremendously. He has a way of shaking it off,
the essence of which is his unharmed belief in the universal power of good. An optimist, indeed. Someone who

The Crucifixion of Peter. According to the legend, the disciple asked to be crucified upside-down, feeling unworthy of dying exactly the same way Jesus did. Painting by Caravaggio, 1601.

loves life so much that he sees the light of it and not its shadows.

When victimized by other people, and that happens frequently, he doesn't feel like a victim. When exposed to envy or even hate, he sees beyond it and pities the people who are so aggravated. He may even blame himself, but not for long. He has trust in all of mankind, whatever reality might whip him with.

In a Tarot reading, this card indicates a sacrifice, maybe even a big one, but it will not be harmful at length. You will come out of it on top. Like they say: what doesn't kill you makes you stronger, and in this case happier, too.

A. E. Waite's description
Wisdom, circumspection, discernment, trials, sacrifice, intuition, divination, prophecy. Reversed: Selfishness, the crowd, body politic.

DEATH.

13   Death

A costly loss
– sometimes, but not always,
the death of someone.

Death is, no doubt, the most terrifying of the Tarot cards to get at a reading. Therefore, guides to the Tarot usually point out that it's not necessarily about death, but some significant loss, change, or revelation. Well, it's about death, too. That's part of life.

I've had Death appear just a few times in my Tarot readings, but in those cases it has proven to be about real death, or at least something almost as sinister. Not my own death – yet – but one happening in my surroundings or the surroundings of the person I did the reading for.

We have to respect the simple fact that life has its horrors. Therefore, so do all methods of divination. If we want to peek into the future, everything isn't going to be good news. We have to prepare for that, before trying any system of divination.

Just looking at the card gives a hint of its grimness. Death on a white horse, black flag in hand, people mourning beside a corpse. The bishop, too, indicates that something definite and shocking has happened. It could be the scene after a battle, an accident, or a plague ravaging the country.

Death catching a pedlar. Illustration from Dance of Death by Hans Holbein the Younger, 1526. Portraying Death as a skeleton started in the 15th century and soon became the norm. Artist around that time made many such pictures, with the basic message that nobody escapes death.

But the sun in the background reveals that life will go on, anyway. The child in the picture gives the same message.

Death is part of life. We're born, so we will die one day. Although it's the very first rule of existence, it's the most difficult one to come to terms with. That's why we tend to be shocked when death appears – in our lives or as a card in a Tarot reading. It's as if we pretend it can be escaped by being ignored. But the only way of learning to live with it is to accept it.

That said, the Death card is not always about physical death, although that can be the case. It can also indicate a drastic change including a costly loss, a painful farewell, and things of that kind. It's sure to be difficult and the change is lasting. The situation after this event is quite different and will not be reversible. So, it's always a death of sorts.

Note that this ill-aboding card has the number 13, which is feared in Christian tradition. This number as the unlucky one stems from the number of disciples of Jesus: they were twelve and, until his devilish betrayal, a thirteenth: Judas.

A. E. Waite's description
End, mortality, destruction, corruption, also, for a man, the loss of a benefactor, for a woman, many contrarieties; for a maid, failure of marriage projects. Reversed: Inertia, sleep, lethargy, petrifaction, somnambulism; hope destroyed.

14 Temperance

Moderation in all
is ultimate persistence.

The simple explanation of Temperance is moderation, but there's nothing simple about it. This quality is regarded as the finest of all in just about every philosophy and religion of the world, all through time. Living modestly, with patience and contemplation, brings life into balance. That is what perseveres.

The oldest and most consistent philosophy of temperance is that of Taoism, as described by Lao Tzu around 2,500 years ago. He called it *wu-wei*, non-action, and insisted that the universe always returns to perfect balance if left alone. So, don't rock the boat.

But Lao Tzu was far from alone in praising moderation. Jesus was quite firm about it, stating that only those who are able to refrain from greed and excess can find the way to Heaven. Buddha was even more extreme about it, saying that one must resist every temptation, every engagement in the worldly, in order to escape the treadmill that is life.

Actually, everywhere we go to find ancient wisdom about how to live our lives, the message is the same. Temperance.

The Ecstasy of Saint Therese. Painting by Francesco Fontebasso, 18th century. The ecstasy in question is a religious one, a popular motif in Christian art. Angels are often portrayed as inspiring forebearance, calming victims of life's hardships and helping them to accept their fate.

Yin and Yang. Ink painting by the author.

The most famous symbol of what the Temperance card speaks of is yin and yang, the Chinese circle of polarities, where black and white embrace into a whole. In traditional Chinese cosmology, these two fundamental forces and the dynamics between them are what made the whole universe emerge.

Let's look at the picture on the Temperance Tarot card. The splendid angel pours water between cups. That's the ultimate image of balance. As Lao Tzu pointed out: Water always floats to the lowest place, thereby creating and keeping balance through modesty. Emphasizing this fundamental lesson to be learned from water, the

Saint Francis meditating. Panting by El Greco, c. 1595. El Greco also made other versions of this motif, which seems to have brought him solace. The meditation of this Medieval friar was quite different from Eastern techniques that we now know of, but still gave him peace of mind through his faith in Christ. Therefore, his eyes are on the crucifix.

angel stands with one foot in it, and the other on land. Also the triangle on the angel's chest, each of its three sides and angles the same size, speaks of balance on a divine level.

Moderation leads to balance, but it's a delicate thing to reach and to sustain. We can see this on the concentration of the angel and the risk of water spilling from the cups. Patience is needed. So is extreme sensitivity. You need to tread lightly, speak softly, and refrain from using any force, no matter how tempting it is when you approach the goal.

If the card refers to a person, it's someone with the quality of temperance – the ability to patiently await the solution and never try to rush it.

If the card indicates an event, it advices extreme caution, because the final outcome is not what appears first. If you have the patience to wait, your reward will be sweet and lasting.

A. E. Waite's description
Economy, moderation, frugality, management, accommodation. Reversed: Things connected with churches, religions, sects, the priesthood, sometimes even the priest who will marry the Querent; also disunion, unfortunate combinations, competing interests.

15 The Devil

The pain and delight
of giving in to temptation.

This devil is all about temptation and how we're often enslaved by our lust. There are many other devils, pointing to other vices and weaknesses of mankind. This one focuses on sexual aspects, which makes it much less frightening.

At the time of the production of this Tarot card deck, the beginning of the 20th century, lust was generally regarded as a sin, and sex was shameful – at least out of wedlock. Times have changed, though not completely and not everywhere. Still, modern society usually has a much brighter view on the sexual urges and their satisfaction than what the picture on this card implies.

There are indeed many devils, in such a way that the ideas about what the devil signifies varies through time as well as from one congregation to another.

The fallen angel of the Old Testament usually tried to expose people as not being that very devoted to their god. Sin was to deviate from the path man was supposed to travel. When the praise of chastity grew in the monasteries, as a way of remaining faithful to God, so did the condemnation of lust and sex. A good Christian was sup-

Pan and Daphnis. Roman copy of a Hellenistic sculpture.

posed to deny carnal instincts and become spiritual, almost as if leaving the body already in this life.

In such a world, the devil would be the one tempting people to give in to their carnal desires. But there have been different views on the devil as well as on what is sin.

Goethe in his *Faust* made the devil a clever guy who revealed people's hypocrisy, thereby sort of doing God's work. Occultists in the early 20th century and onwards, such as Aleister Crowley of The Golden Dawn, saw the devil as a representation of the necessity to liberate oneself of inhibitions, in order to realize one's full potential as a human being. That devil was a challenger.

In comparative religion, the devil is definitely what's called a trickster, a divinity acting as sort of a mediator between gods and men, often working for the benefit of the latter against the will of the former. A revolutionary of sorts.

But back to the devil portrayed on this Tarot card. He sits like a ruler of the enchained woman and man, who also have horns on their heads, albeit small ones. That makes them willfully enchained – two persons giving in to their temptations.

The card should be compared to that of the Lovers, who are guarded by an angel and who seem to remain in chastity. It's Eros against Agape – carnal love against spiritual. This Tarot deck condemns the former and praises the latter. But life would cease to exist without both.

So, the Devil is not necessarily a card about evil things happening. It's about temptation and satisfaction, lust and passion and boundless delight. It's about challenging

Hell, the third panel of the triptych The Garden of Earthly Delights, by Hieronymus Bosch, around 1500.

one's limitations and inhibitions, daring to question established morals, revolting against prejudice.

When the card represents a person, it's somebody doing just that. When it represents an event, it's an opportunity to do that.

In short, the card asks the question: Do you dare to fall for your temptation, and if not – do you have the strength to resist it?

As for the image of the devil, which we are quite familiar with, its inspiration is bound to come from Greek and Roman mythical creatures, such as Pan, the Fauns, and Satyrs. The horns are there, the goat legs too. Also, Pan and the others are notoriously lustful and uninhibited in the myths – the very opposite of what the Bible seems to preach.

A. E. Waite's description
Ravage, violence, vehemence, extraordinary efforts, force, fatality; that which is predestined but is not for this reason evil. Reversed: Evil fatality, weakness, pettiness, blindness.

THE TOWER.

16 The Tower

A spectacular ambition
that ends with disaster.

The Tower is evidently a card indicating disaster. The picture shows that clearly. But what leads to the disaster? One legendary tower explains it – that of Babel, surely inspiring both the image and the meaning of this Tarot card.

Babel was built to reach heaven. This megalomania angered God, who crushed the tower completely – and made people strangers to one another, so that they would never be able to repeat the feat.

The flash from the dark sky is God's anger, and the people who fall from its height are punished for their hubris, comparing themselves to God by wanting to reach his abode. The crown thrown off the top of the tower is the symbol of utter human vanity. Great plans invite great failures. If the plan is too great, failure is certain. We invite it by aiming far too high.

On the other hand, what's the point of being human if not pushing the limits, aiming as high as we can ever imagine? If we never did, we would still be running from saber-toothed tigers somewhere in the wilderness. Our fantasy compels us to pursue our dreams. Sometimes it

The Tower of Babel. Painting by Pieter Bruegel the Elder, 1563

leads to disaster, sometimes to wonderful success. So, how can we stop ourselves?

If this card relates to a person, it's someone capable of destroying things that seem as solid as mountains, and hurrying to do so. It's the destructive instinct. Although costly, it's necessary in the grand scheme of things. What goes up must come down, and someone has to make sure of it.

If the card refers to an event, it's the unfortunate end to an ambitious project. Failure. Probably, you aimed too high and lifted a weight that was far too heavy. It couldn't last. Should you insist on your ambitious goal, you must be prepared to do it all over from the start, and there will be additional obstacles to overcome.

A. E. Waite's description
Misery, distress, indigence, adversity, calamity, disgrace, deception, ruin. It is a card in particular of unforeseen catastrophe. Reversed: According to one account, the same in a lesser degree, also oppression, imprisonment, tyranny.

THE STAR.

17   The Star

Time to pause and reflect,
contemplate what's precious and what's not.

The Star is very distant and mysterious. Although the sky on the image is light blue, the Star is a nocturnal being. Its shimmering light inspires contemplation and dreaming. It's emotion is melancholia. You need to pause and ponder what existence is all about.

Don't expect this card to answer questions. Instead, it raises new ones – or old ones that you've forgotten because you were so occupied with worldly matters, ambitious plans, and what-not. Who doesn't become somber and thoughtful when watching the stars in the night sky? All that mattered so much seems to lose importance and attraction.

The Star is about emotions, which is indicated by all the water on the image, poured serenely by the woman. The element water represents the emotional. But these feelings lead to stillness, and the stillness leads to thoughts.

What moves through our heads when we are at rest, not involved in all those things that make a lifetime pass so swiftly? That's what the Star urges us to explore. If we never do, it's like we never lived.

A traveler at the edge of the firmament, the Medieval concept of the starry sky as a dome covering the earth. The illustration is often mistakenly believed to be of renaissance origin, but it comes from The Atmosphere: Popular Meteorology, by Camille Flammarion, 1888.

If the Tarot card represents a person, it's someone inspiring reflection, making you ponder where you are in life and where you really want to go.

If the card represents an event, it's a moment when things halt so that you have time to reconsider, which you should. Goals are questioned. So are values previously upheld. You should sit down and meditate, until you're open to completely new perspectives.

A. E. Waite's description

Loss, theft, privation, abandonment; another reading says hope and bright prospects, Reversed: Arrogance, haughtiness, impotence.

THE MOON .

18 The Moon

Longing for the sake of longing,
and the hope of fulfillment.

The Moon card stands for longing, the needs of the soul, just like the moon does in astrology. The link to astrology, older by far than the Tarot, is obvious in several ways on the card's image. Mainly, the sign of which the moon is the ruler, Cancer, is suggested by the water as well as the crayfish – the element and the original symbol of this Zodiac sign.

Ancient astrology is a primary source to just about every system of symbols and metaphysical thinking. The Major Arcana of the Tarot deck has three cards particularly connected to the components of astrology: the Moon, the Sun, and the Star. The first two are present in any horoscope, whereas the third one can be said to represent the astral perspective as such.

The Moon, the nocturnal light, is what moves within us. It represents what we long for and need to be satisfied at depth. Cravings of the Moon are not silenced by one single feast, no matter how spectacular. They are constant reminders from within.

When we're unable to satisfy these needs, we get frustrated, at length maddeningly so. At moments when we

The Moon (represented by the Roman goddess Luna on her chariot) and its astrological traits. Woodcut by Hans Sebald Beham, from the 1530's.

do please our inner longings, we're at peace for a while, just to have our thirst increase in no time. It takes its toll, but what can you do?

The canines barking at the moon show the power of the urge and the difficulty of solving it. They bark at what they can't reach. In one way or other, we all do. Longing is a paradox. If we reach what we long for, our longing should stop – but it doesn't. It's because we need to long for something or other. Without longing we become complacent, passive, as if sleeping.

In divination, if the Moon card refers to a person, it's somebody who awakens your longing by seeming able to fulfill it. But as said above, that's not the likely outcome. Instead, your longing will probably be increased, which is not at all a bad thing, although frustrating.

If the card refers to an event, it's a moment when your longing is obvious to you and things happen that increase it. It can create turmoil of emotions in you, but you welcome it – albeit with some trepidation. At the very least, you're reminded of your emotional needs and the importance of trying to satisfy them.

A. E. Waite's description

Hidden enemies, danger, calumny, darkness, terror, deception, occult forces, error. Reversed: Instability, inconstancy, silence, lesser degrees of deception and error.

19 The Sun

Great resources at your disposal,
but constrain yourself
since it's possible to have too much.

The sun brings light and life to our whole planet. It's the source of seemingly endless energy, without which we couldn't exist. The Sun card of the Tarot shows this splendid star of ours, and the abundance it brings. So, it's certainly a fortunate card, if not the very card of fortune as such.

The image on this card suggests the sun on its triumphant return at the vernal equinox, maybe also its zenith in the middle of the summer. The vernal equinox was in the past regarded as the start of the new year, because of how the expanding daylight of spring rejuvenates all of nature. That's implied by the infant greeting us with open arms, as it rides towards us on the white horse.

The proud sunflowers and the sun's central position, with its strong rays in every direction, suggest summer, too. Midsummer, with the longest day and the shortest night of all the year. The sun at the peak of its power.

The sun is the great nourisher, but its force can be terrible if not respected. It's pure power, beyond any intent of good or bad. It just is, and all of us reached by its light

Sonn.

The Sun (represented by the Greek god Helios on his chariot) and its astrological traits. Woodcut by Hans Sebald Beham, from the 1530's. The sun as a god on a chariot, traveling daily across the sky, exists in many mythologies.

prosper from it. A resource that's not spent, no matter how much it's used. Yet, an indifferent one, so it allows itself to be used for whatever purpose. That's not without risk.

Of course, a resource of that magnitude is hazardous. It should be used with some moderation, or its power might be destructive. But if received humbly and gratefully, it brings joy and well-being.

In divination, if the Sun card represents a person, it's someone extremely resourceful and willing to help. But don't accept more than you need and can handle, or there may be dire consequences. That person has no obligation at all to serve you, so don't strain his or her patience.

If the card represents an event, it's a golden opportunity. Things happen from which you can prosper tremendously. But still, limit your greed, consider what you really need and what would be gluttony. A good fortune can be just as difficult to handle as a bad one.

A. E. Waite's description
Material happiness, fortunate marriage, contentment. Reversed: The same in a lesser sense.

JUDGEMENT.

20 Judgment

Ultimate judgment,
whether we welcome it or not.

The picture on the Judgment card makes no secret about what judgment it refers to: the Last Judgment, when all the people who ever lived are awakened and sent either to Heaven or to Hell for eternity. Ultimate justice. Sublime reward for the good and terrible punishment for the bad. This moment is also the one of the end of the world as we know it.

At such cost, is it really justice we want?

To countless Christians through the past two thousand years, the idea of divine justice had wonderful appeal, since so many of them were constantly victims of injustice.

It started already by their savior being crucified and many of his disciples meeting a similar fate. And the first generation of Christians in Rome was hunted down by the forces of a vicious Emperor.

They dreamed of the Last Judgment and prayed that it was near.

This Tarot card, then, signals the promise of justice being done, eventually. The villains will be revealed and the righteous ones will be rewarded. At a cost.

The Last Judgment, by Stefan Lochner c. 1435. This painting is made in a style that is quite Medieval, where the sizes of the figures indicate their importance. Notice that the entrance to Paradise looks very much like a church, whereas the entrance to the lower regions is more like a castle of a worldly ruler.

(Bottom left) The Last Judgment, by Hans Memling 1473. In this triptych, the separation of souls is done in the middle. The entrance to Paradise is through the cathedral to the left, but the way to Hell is simply to be thrown into the fire on the right. The style of the painting is still quite Medieval, with a limited depth of perspective and sizes according to importance. Christ, with the marks of his crucifixion, is heading the event, almost as if involved in vengeance.

The Last Judgment, by Michelangelo 1541. This is part of Michelangelo's decoration of the Sistine Chapel. Here, Christ acts on his own, involved in the actual deed. (cont.)

(continuing from previous page) Mother Mary is a grieving witness. Jesus is not significally bigger than the others, but holds center stage. It's not altogether clear who goes to Heaven and who to Hell. Everyone seems to suffer. Michelangelo focuses on the tragedy of it all, whatever justice might dictate.

The Last Judgment, by Peter Paul Rubens, 1617. Jesus' gesture and the composition of the painting reveal an influence from Michelangelo, but here the tragedy is overshadowed by the spectacle. Rubens treats the subject lustfully.

Tarot

A Vision of the Last Judgment, by William Blake 1808. Blake's image is that of the spectacle in itself (much like Rubens treats it), regardless of right and wrong. Christ at the top is like a statue, passive as if as much a victim as everybody else. At the left, people go up towards Heaven, at the left they go down towards Hell. The whole picture becomes a clockwise circular movement. Who's to say what's right or wrong? Blake just marvels at the glory of it all.

Judgment is final and irrevocable. That's dire in itself. Is it really what we want? Furthermore, are we that sure of being innocent and the others are the only guilty ones?

If we call for Judgment it will come, and it will strike according to its own elevated perception. The outcome is never certain, no matter how we might have convinced ourselves of the opposite. So, it's a moment of fear for the good and the bad alike.

This Tarot card has sort of a twin in that of Justice, which seems just as clear about the right and the wrong of things, but at closer inspection reveals the complexity of it all. But Justice is not definite, since it's of the world. Judgment, though, is forever.

There may be a reason for our legal system preferring Justice to Judgment.

When this card relates to a person, it means that he or she is very judgmental and not inclined to change his or her mind about it. In the eyes of somebody with that characteristic, few people pass.

When the card relates to an event, it means that a final judgment will arrive and there is nothing anyone can do about it.

Judgment Day is a spectacular vision, which has inspired many artists through the centuries, especially in the long period when the church was their richest and most frequent client. The previous pages have some of the paintings on the theme. On the Internet you can easily find them in larger versions – and you want to do that, because these are scenes surpassing anything Hollywood manages even with the biggest budgets.

A. E. Waite's description
Change of position, renewal, outcome. Another account specifies total loss though lawsuit. Reversed: Weakness, pusillanimity, simplicity; also deliberation, decision, sentence.

21 The World

Success in anything worldly,
but not for free.

The World is a place of infinite opportunity, there for the grabbing. You can conquer it and you can lose it. The Tarot card opens this vast resource, but who has an embrace wide enough to encompass it?

Everything has a price. Jesus warned about gaining the whole world and losing one's soul in the process. The Tarot card repeats the warning by having the four beasts of the Apocalypse in the corners: a lion, a calf, a man, and an eagle. They are also the symbols of the four Evangelists Mark, Luke, Matthew, and John.

So, if you strive for the world as your oyster, heed the warnings. You can get anything at a cost, but if you crave everything – that costs a lot. Success takes its toll.

Many people still don't hesitate, but go for it, happily forgetting about the price until they're handed the bill. Then they realize that they should have halted and eaten moderately from the buffet. Although you may at times be offered the world, curb your enthusiasm and ask yourself how much of it you really need.

If just handled calmly and with some restraint, the opportunity that this Tarot card promises is splendid.

Christ surrounded by the representations of the four evangelists: Matthew (a man), John (an eagle), Mark (a lion), and Luke (a calf). Coffin cover from the 13th century.

Success in whatever worldly matter is at hand. When the World card relates to an event, it opens up plenty of possibilities beyond your initial expectation. But be careful with your choices.

If the card relates to a person, it's someone who can offer success on a silver platter – but watch out for the price tag. There is one, although it might not be evident at first. If the deal is too good to be true, it's probably not.

So, this card, although overwhelmingly generous, propagates moderation, as does the very archetype of that virtue, the card of Temperance. When you can get everything in abundance, beware.

A. E. Waite's description

Assured success, recompense, voyage, route, emigration, flight, change of place. Reversed: Inertia, fixity, stagnation, permanence.

O

THE FOOL .

0   The Fool

Blissful carelessness,
the power of ignorance.

He may be a fool, but doesn't he look happy? Maybe that's what it takes to be joyous in this world: ignorance is bliss.

This is my favorite Tarot card. Looking at it, I get a sense of his happiness, which makes me smile. It's the introverted happiness, and that's the most difficult one to obtain. If you're happy when you're on your own, then you are truly happy, at peace with yourself. This fool must have made it, because he look euphoric. Indeed, this character is the personification of euphoria.

There are many kinds of happiness, most of them short lived, ending in the gloom that their departure induces. But this Fool has found something lasting – a joy that emerges from deep inside, seemingly for no reason at all. He has discovered that deep inside, he's content. Such happiness remains and is easy to return to.

The dog by his side can feel the authenticity of his happiness and that it's just as unconditional as canine love. So, of course they join.

Well, the dog does. The fool is too inebriated by his joy to notice anything around him. He's by the edge of a

The Ecstasy of Saint Theresa. Sculpture by Gian Lorenzo Bernini, 1652. The religious ecstasy may be something other than euphoria, but there are similarities. Artists enjoyed pointing them out, also occasionally adding what seems to be a hint at another overwhelming rush of joy – that of the orgasm.

The Ecstasy of Saint Paul. Painting by Nicolas Poussin, 1650.
The usually somber apostle looks almost indecently joyous and
carefree on this picture, for a change. Carried by angels and not
a worry in the world. That's the spirit of the Fool.

cliff, his face turned to the sky. But it seems that if he takes another step, he will not fall. He'll probably just keep on walking – in mid-air, like cartoon figures.

This card definitely indicates happiness. Whatever problem there was, it's gone as if all by itself, leaving you carefree. Other threats might appear, but they'll not damage the one who doesn't worry. The cure is always to never cease taking delight in life.

Note that A. E. Waite and others assigned the number 0 to this card, although it's the 22nd. For the Fool, that seems appropriate.

A. E. Waite's description
Folly, mania, extravagance, intoxication, delirium, frenzy, bewrayment. Reversed: Negligence, absence, distribution, carelessness, apathy, nullity, vanity.

The Minor Arcana

The four Suits of the Tarot Card Deck

The Tarot card deck consists of two parts – the Major Arcana (also called Trumps) with 22 cards and the Minor Arcana with the remaining 56 cards in four suits: Wands, Pentacles, Cups, and Swords. Here the four suits are presented, followed by all their cards and what they mean in divination.

The Minor Arcana is close to regular playing card decks, but with one card extra in each suit: the Page. So, each suit has 14 cards from Ace to King. Also, each suit represents its own perspective on life, indicated by the symbol of that suit.

Apart from my own short suggestions for the card meanings, I've added A. E. Waite's description of each card, since he was the one designing them, and his keywords for how they should be interpreted. I should add that I don't always agree with the latter.

Wands

Wands correspond to Clubs in a regular deck of cards. Their Greek element is earth. They stand for everything earthbound and concrete. In the four classes of feudal society, this suit was linked to that of agriculture, the peasants.

When a Wands card appears in a reading, its message is concrete: something to do or something done, work and struggle but also their reward in palpable results.

Here are the 14 cards of the Wands suit and what they mean in Tarot card divination.

Ace of Wands

Every Ace is sort of an exclamation mark. Something important, even remarkable, will take place – in the case of Wands regarding your material circumstances. It's neither good nor bad, but very significant, indeed, affecting your relation to material matters.

A. E. Waite's description:

A hand issuing from a cloud grasps a stout wand or club.

A. E. Waite's keywords:

Calamities of all kinds. Reversed: A sign of birth.

2 of Wands

Longing for the world and all it has to offer, although you may already have a decent share of it.

A. E. Waite's description:

A tall man looks from a battlemented roof over sea and shore; he holds a globe in his right hand, while a staff in his left rests on the battlement; another is fixed in a ring. The Rose and Cross and Lily should be noticed on the left side.

A. E. Waite's keywords:

A young lady may expect trivial disappointments.

3 of Wands

Missing the world and all the good things it has offered. The card of having partaken in something rewarding, but now being passed by, as if obsolete.

A. E. Waite's description:

A calm, stately personage, with his back turned, looking from a cliff's edge at ships passing over the sea. Three staves are planted in the ground, and he leans slightly on one of them.

A. E. Waite's keywords:

A very good card; collaboration will favor enterprise.

4 of Wands

The celebration of a homecoming of sorts. Returning from the world, enriched and pleased, receiving the praise and rewards for it.

A. E. Waite's description:

From the four great staves planted in the foreground there is a great garland suspended; two female figures uplift nosegays; at their side is a bridge over a moat, leading to an old manorial house.

A. E. Waite's keywords:

Unexpected good fortune. Reversed: A married woman will have beautiful children.

5 of Wands

Calamity that may be invigorating but can become costly. What seems easy at first turns complicated when ambitions collide.

A. E. Waite's description:

A posse of youths, who are brandishing staves, as if in sport or strife. It is mimic warfare.

A. E. Waite's keywords:

Success in financial speculation. Reversed: Quarrels may be turned to advantage.

6 of Wands

Success and great gain in material matters, making others want to join you. But don't forget to prepare for rainy days that may come.

A. E. Waite's description:

A laurelled horseman bears one staff adorned with a laurel crown; footmen with staves are at his side.

A. E. Waite's keywords:

Servants may lose the confidence of their masters; a young lady may be betrayed by a friend. Reversed: Fulfillment of deferred hope.

7 of Wands

Struggle to hold on to what you have. Others try to take it from you.

A. E. Waite's description:

A young man on a craggy eminence brandishing a staff; six other staves are raised towards him from below.

A. E. Waite's keywords:

A dark child.

8 of Wands

Possessions on the move, risking to get lost. Hard work that is costly but necessary, to overcome several concrete obstacles.

A. E. Waite's description:

The card represents motion through the immovable – a flight of wands through an open country; but they draw to the term of their course. That which they signify is at hand; it may be even on the threshold.

A. E. Waite's keywords:

Domestic disputes for a married person.

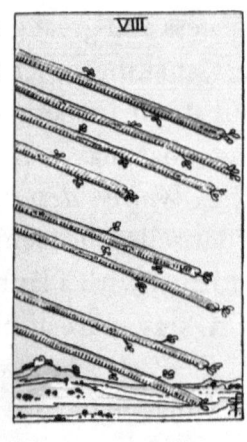

9 of Wands

Recovering after having been over-whelmed by too many disadvantages. You struggled hard, but everything was against you. You want to try again.

A. E. Waite's description:
The figure leans upon his staff and has an expectant look, as if awaiting an enemy. Behind are eight other staves – erect, in orderly disposition, like a palisade.

A. E. Waite's keywords:
Generally speaking, a bad card.

10 of Wands

Too much to carry. Your workload is unreasonable, and still there's no certain reward ahead. Are you being used for others' profit?

A. E. Waite's description:
A man oppressed by the weight of the ten staves which he is carrying.

A. E. Waite's keywords:
Difficulties and contradictions, if near a good card.

Page of Wands

Plenty of possibilities, so many that it's difficult to choose. Do something, and you will prosper. But wait no longer.

A. E. Waite's description:

In a scene similar to the former, a young man stands in the act of proclamation. He is unknown but faithful, and his tidings are strange.

A. E. Waite's keywords:

Young man of family in search of young lady. Reversed: Bad news.

Knight of Wands

You have grasped the opportunity and boldly move forward. Great promises of success, as long as you just sit tightly on your saddle.

A. E. Waite's description:

He is shown as if upon a journey, armed with a short wand, and although mailed is not on a warlike errand. He is passing mounds or pyramids. The motion of the horse is a key to the character of its rider, and sug-gests the precipitate mood, or things connected therewith.

A. E. Waite's keywords:

A bad card; according to some readings, alienation. Reversed: For a woman, marriage, but probably frustrated.

Queen of Wands

You have your possessions and know how to keep them, but do you know how to increase them? Don't settle with what you have, or it may wither.

A. E. Waite's description:

The Wands throughout this suit are always in leaf, as it is a suit of life and animation. Emotionally and other- wise, the Queen's personality corre- sponds to that of the King, but is more magnetic.

A. E. Waite's keywords:

A good harvest, which may be taken in several senses. Reversed: Goodwill towards the Querent, but without the opportunity to exercise it.

King of Wands

Wealth that is hard to keep. What's the point of prosperity if you don't trust that you can hold on to it? Envy is a poison also to the object of it.

A. E. Waite's description:

The King uplifts a flowering wand, and wears what is called a cap of maintenance beneath his crown. He connects with the symbol of the lion, which is embla- zoned on the back of his throne.

A. E. Waite's keywords:

Generally favorable, may signify a good marriage. Re- versed: Advice that should be followed.

Pentacles

Pentacles correspond to Diamonds in a regular deck of cards. Their Greek element is air. They stand for monetary matters, everything about economy, but also thought, communication and other things of the mind. In the four classes of feudal society, this suit was linked to that of trade, merchants and businessmen.

When a Pentacles card appears in a reading, its message regards matters of economy, but also thoughts, study, plans – anything abstract, present in the mind but not yet in one's hands, either not yet or, because of its nature, never.

Here are the 14 cards of the Pentacles suit and what they mean in Tarot card divination.

Ace of Pentacles

This card is like an exclamation mark. An idea is forming, demanding contemplation. It can lead to a lot of good things.

A. E. Waite's description:
A hand – issuing, as usual, from a cloud – holds up a pentacle.

A. E. Waite's keywords:
The most favorable of all cards. Reversed: A share in the finding of treasure.

2 of Pentacles

Confusion. Your mind struggles with trying to make two seeming opposites combine. A paradox that appears insoluble, but it needs not be.

A. E. Waite's description:
A young man, in the act of dancing, has a pentacle in either hand, and they are joined by that endless cord which is like the number 8 reversed.

A. E. Waite's keywords:
Troubles are more imaginary than real. Reversed: Bad omen, ignorance, injustice.

3 of Pentacles

Is it for real or not? You wonder about something essential, unable to know where to find the answer.

A. E. Waite's description:

A sculptor at his work in a monastery. Compare the design which illustrates the Eight of Pentacles. The apprentice or amateur therein has received his reward and is now at work in earnest.

A. E. Waite's keywords:

If for a man, celebrity for his eldest son. Reversed: Depends on neighboring cards.

4 of Pentacles

A self-obsessed mind, caught by the brilliance of his own thinking. But thoughts can be shared without wasting them.

A. E. Waite's description:

A crowned figure, having a pentacle over his crown, clasps another with hands and arms; two pentacles are under his feet. He holds to that which he has.

A. E. Waite's keywords:

For a bachelor, pleasant news from a lady. Reversed: Observation, hindrances.

5 of Pentacles

Desolation. You have no idea how to get out of it, because you're stuck in old lines of thought.

A. E. Waite's description:
Two mendicants in a snow-storm pass a lighted casement.

A. E. Waite's keywords:
Conquest of fortune by reason. Reversed: Troubles in love.

6 of Pentacles

Generosity is easy when done with a surplus. Still, it does good if done with proper modesty.

A. E. Waite's description:
A person in the guise of a merchant weighs money in a pair of scales and distributes it to the needy and distressed. It is a testimony to his own success in life, as well as to his goodness of heart.

A. E. Waite's keywords:
The present must not be relied on. Reversed: A check on the Querent's ambition.

7 of Pentacles

Time for contemplation, which will lead to splendid ideas, Once they're ripe, these ideas will create prosperity.

A. E. Waite's description:

A young man, leaning on his staff, looks intently at seven pentacles attached to a clump of greenery on his right; one would say that these were his treasures and that his heart was there.

A. E. Waite's keywords:

Improved position for a lady's future husband. Reversed: Impatience, apprehension, suspicion.

8 of Pentacles

Work on the plan, think things through. You'll prosper to the extent you take the trouble of being well prepared.

A. E. Waite's description:

An artist in stone at his work, which he exhibits in the form of trophies.

A. E. Waite's keywords:

A young man in business who has relations with the Querent; a dark girl. Reversed: The Querent will be compromised in a matter of money-lending.

9 of Pentacles

Prosperity in so many ways. Time to lean back and enjoy the wealth, primarily the pride of having reached it.

A. E. Waite's description:

A woman, with a bird upon her wrist, stands amidst a great abundance of grapevines in the garden of a manorial house. It is a wide domain, suggesting plenty in all things. Possibly it is her own possession and testifies to material well-being.

A. E. Waite's keywords:

Prompt fulfillment of what is presaged by neighboring cards. Reversed: Vain hopes.

10 of Pentacles

Intellectual stimulation. Wisdom, knowledge, and the exchange of those with inspirational people.

A. E. Waite's description:

A man and woman beneath an archway which gives entrance to a house and domain. They are accompanied by a child, who looks curiously at two dogs accosting an ancient personage seated in the foreground. The child's hand is on one of them.

A. E. Waite's keywords:

Represents house or dwelling, and derives its value from other cards. Reversed: An occasion which may be fortunate or otherwise.

Page of Pentacles

Time to dream and let the fantasy go. That invigorates and opens for new possibilities. Be optimistic.

A. E. Waite's description:

A youthful figure, looking intently at the pentacle which hovers over his raised hands. He moves slowly, insensible of that which is about him.

A. E. Waite's keywords:

A dark youth; a young officer or soldier; a child. Reversed: Sometimes degradation and sometimes pillage.

Knight of Pentacles

Follow a course, stick to the plan, and you can reach even a far-fetched goal. You just need resolution.

A. E. Waite's description:

He rides a slow, enduring, heavy horse, to which his own aspect corresponds. He exhibits his symbol, but does not look therein.

A. E. Waite's keywords:

An useful man; useful discoveries. Reversed: A brave man out of employment.

Queen of Pentacles

Pondering, unable to get out of it. It's all too serious. But such times are also needed, for personal growth.

A. E. Waite's description:

The face suggests that of a dark woman, whose qualities might be summed up in the idea of greatness of soul; she has also the serious cast of intelligence; she contemplates her symbol and may see worlds therein.

A. E. Waite's keywords:

Dark woman; presents from a rich relative; rich and happy marriage for a young man. Reversed: An illness.

King of Pentacles

Thinking ahead is the way to ascertain what was gained in the past. The key to success is holding on to it.

A. E. Waite's description:

The figure calls for no special description, the face is rather dark, suggesting also courage, but somewhat lethargic in tendency. The bull's head should be noted as a recurrent symbol on the throne.

A. E. Waite's keywords:

A rather dark man, a merchant, master, professor. Reversed: An old and vicious man.

Cups

Cups correspond to Hearts in a regular deck of cards. Their Greek element is water. They stand for everything emotional – what we feel, whether or not we actually live it. In the four classes of feudal society, this suit was linked to that of the clergy, since the church and religion is all about emotions.

When a Cups card appears in a reading, its message is always about things of an emotional nature: Worries, delights, temptations, hopes, affections, disappointments, and so on. The events or situations that primarily affect the heart.

Here are the 14 cards of the Cups suit and what they mean in Tarot card divination.

Ace of Cups

The Ace is an exclamation mark. Now, it's all about feelings. Solace. Bliss is around the corner.

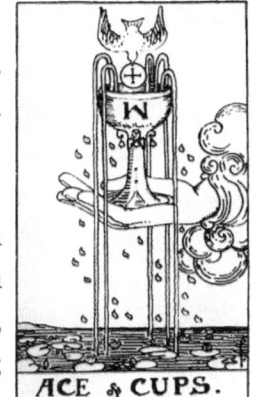

A. E. Waite's description:

The waters are beneath, and thereon are water-lilies; the hand issues from the cloud, holding in its palm the cup, from which four streams are pouring; a dove, bearing in its bill a cross-marked Host, descends to place the Wafer in the Cup; the dew of water is falling on all sides.

A. E. Waite's keywords:

Inflexible will, unalterable law. Reversed: Unexpected change of position.

2 of Cups

Partners, companions, lovers. Whatever the bond, there's great pleasure in sharing with another.

A. E. Waite's description:

A youth and maiden are pledging one another, and above their cups rises the Caduceus of Hermes, between the great wings of which there appears a lion's head.

A. E. Waite's keywords:

Favorable in things of pleasure and business, as well as love; also wealth and honor. Reversed: Passion.

3 of Cups

Celebration in the merry company of dear friends. A time to remember.

A. E. Waite's description:

Maidens in a garden-ground with cups uplifted, as if pledging one another.

A. E. Waite's keywords:

Unexpected advancement for a military man. Reversed: Consolation, cure, end of the business.

4 of Cups

Dissatisfaction. When you've had enough, what can pleasure you next? The question that brings on melancholia.

A. E. Waite's description:

A young man is seated under a tree and contemplates three cups set on the grass before him; an arm issuing from a cloud offers him another cup. His expression notwithstanding is one of discontent with his environment.

A. E. Waite's keywords:

Contrarieties. Reversed: Presentiment.

5 of Cups

Despair. Life lost its taste, there's no remedy against gloom – but accepting it. It will dissolve, eventually.

A. E. Waite's description:

A dark, cloaked figure, looking sideways at three prone cups, two others stand upright behind him; a bridge is in the background, leading to a small keep or holding.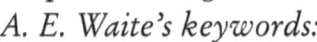

A. E. Waite's keywords:

Generally favorable; a happy marriage; also patrimony, legacies, gifts, success in enterprise. Reversed: Return of some relative who has not been seen for long.

6 of Cups

Joy and childish happiness. Nothing seems complicated, no threats are imminent. Cherish the moment.

A. E. Waite's description:

Children in an old garden, their cups filled with flowers.

A. E. Waite's keywords:

Pleasant memories. Reversed: Inheritance to fall in quickly.

7 of Cups

How to resist temptation, how to still the longing for everything in the world? That which you want is a mirage.

A. E. Waite's description:
Strange chalices of vision, but the images are more, especially those of the fantastic spirit.

A. E. Waite's keywords:
Fair child; idea, design, resolve, movement. Reversed: Success, if accompanied by the Three of Cups.

8 of Cups

Turning away in disgust from having discovered that what seemed so sweet had a bitter aftertaste. But it brings maturity.

A. E. Waite's description:
A man of dejected aspect is deserting the cups of his felicity, enterprise, undertaking or previous concern.

A. E. Waite's keywords:
Marriage with a fair woman. Reversed: Perfect satisfaction.

9 of Cups

Gluttony inflates the mind as well as the body. So does complacency, the gluttony of the mind.

A. E. Waite's description:

A goodly personage has feasted to his heart's content, and abundant refreshment of wine is on the arched counter behind him, seeming to indicate that the future is also assured.

A. E. Waite's keywords:

Of good augury for military men. Reversed: Good business.

10 of Cups

The bliss of accomplishment, when benefitting all involved. The reward of the worthy.

A. E. Waite's description:

Appearance of Cups in a rainbow; it is contemplated in wonder and ecstasy by a man and woman below, evidently husband and wife. His right arm is about her; his left is raised upward;

she raises her right arm. The two children dancing near them have not observed the prodigy but are happy after their own manner. There is a home-scene beyond.

A. E. Waite's keywords:

For a male Querent, a good marriage and one beyond his expectations. Reversed: Sorrow; also a serious quarrel.

Page of Cups

The irony of it all. Funny or sad, when looked at with open eyes anything is amusing. Expect to be surprised.

A. E. Waite's description:

A fair, pleasing, somewhat effeminate page, of studious and intent aspect, contemplates a fish rising from a cup to look at him. It is the pictures of the mind taking form.

A. E. Waite's keywords:

Good augury; also a young man who is unfortunate in love. Reversed: Obstacles of all kinds.

Knight of Cups

Pride makes lousy armor, but we're all even more vulnerable without it. Make sure you do something to be proud of.

A. E. Waite's description:

Graceful, but not warlike; riding quietly, wearing a winged helmet, referring to those higher graces of the imagination which sometimes charac-

terize this card. He too is a dreamer, but the images of the side of sense haunt him in his vision.

A. E. Waite's keywords:

A visit from a friend, who will bring unexpected money to the Querent. Reversed: Irregularity.

Queen of Cups

Stuck in obsession, what the feelings use to trap the mind and vice versa. It's not worth it.

A. E. Waite's description:

Beautiful, fair, dreamy – as one who sees visions in a cup. This is, however, only one of her aspects; she sees, but she also acts, and her activity feeds her dream.

A. E. Waite's keywords:

Sometimes denotes a woman of equivocal character. Reversed: A rich marriage for a man and a distinguished one for a woman.

King of Cups

Nothing wrong with being very pleased, except for flaunting it to induce jealousy. Take nothing for granted, not even yourself.

A. E. Waite's description:

He holds a short scepter in his left hand and a great cup in his right; his throne is set upon the sea; on one side a ship is riding and on the other a dolphin is leaping.

A. E. Waite's keywords:

Beware of ill-will on the part of a man of position, and of hypocrisy pretending to help. Reversed: Loss.

Swords

Swords correspond to Spades in a regular deck of cards. Their Greek element is fire. They stand for forceful action, power, and firm decision. In the four classes of feudal society, this suit is linked to that of the aristocracy, the warriors and rulers.

When a Swords card appears in a reading, its message is about action needed or already commenced, drastic change because of necessity or circumstance, ambition, competition, defense, and other things that demand resolve and bold activity.

Here are the 14 cards of the Swords suit and what they mean in Tarot card divination.

Ace of Swords

This is an exclamation mark, here for the principle of stern action. There is imminent need of it. Do something.

A. E. Waite's description:
A hand issues from a cloud, grasping as word, the point of which is encircled by a crown.

A. E. Waite's keywords:
Great prosperity or great misery. Reversed: Marriage broken off, for a woman, through her own imprudence.

2 of Swords

Where to go when both directions are risky and still haste is called for? You must decide although you can't be sure.

A. E. Waite's description:
A hoodwinked female figure balances two swords upon her shoulders.

A. E. Waite's keywords:
Gifts for a lady, influential protection for a man in search of help. Reversed: Dealings with rogues.

3 of Swords

Does everything work against you, is there no way to go without getting hurt? Take no step before heeding the warning.

A. E. Waite's description:
Three swords piercing a heart; cloud and rain behind.

A. E. Waite's keywords:
For a woman, the flight of her lover. Reversed: A meeting with one whom the Querent has compromised; also a nun.

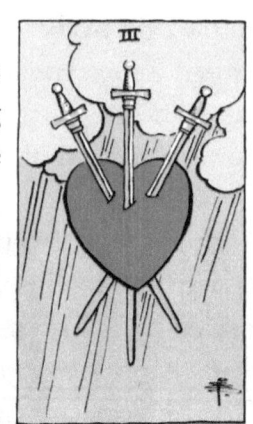

4 of Swords

Not every hero won the battle, but it's still heroic. Treasure how your action will be remembered.

A. E. Waite's description:
The effigy of a knight in the attitude of prayer, at full length upon his tomb.

A. E. Waite's keywords:
A bad card, but if reversed a qualified success may be expected by wise administration of affairs. Reversed: A certain success following wise administration.

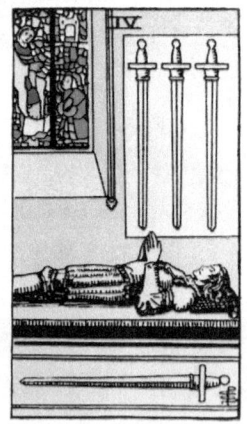

5 of Swords

Betrayal when the battle is over. Time to ask what the battle was really for.

A. E. Waite's description:

A disdainful man looks after two retreating and dejected figures. Their swords lie upon the ground. He carries two others on his left shoulder, and a third sword is in his right hand, point to earth. He is the master in possession of the field.

A. E. Waite's keywords:

An attack on the fortune of the Querent. Reversed: A sign of sorrow and mourning.

6 of Swords

A most costly outcome of a big venture. Either bitter defeat or a Pyrrhic victory. Still, you will persevere.

A. E. Waite's description:

A ferryman carrying passengers in his punt to the further shore. The course is smooth, and seeing that the freight is light, it may be noted that the work is not beyond his strength.

A. E. Waite's keywords:

The voyage will be pleasant. Reversed: Unfavorable issue of lawsuit.

7 of Swords

Betrayal right before the decisive battle. It may not lead to defeat, but victory is suddenly more distant.

A. E. Waite's description:

A man in the act of carrying away five swords rapidly; the two others of the card remain stuck in the ground. A camp is close at hand.

A. E. Waite's keywords:

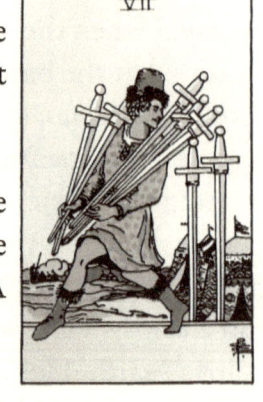

Dark girl; a good card; it promises a country life after a competence has been secured. Reversed: Good advice, probably neglected.

8 of Swords

Helplessly in the hands of others, who seem to show little compassion. Cause for apprehension, but not panic.

A. E. Waite's description:

A woman, bound and hoodwinked, with the swords of the card about her. Yet it is rather a card of temporary durance than of irretrievable bondage.

A. E. Waite's keywords:

For a woman, scandal spread in her respect. Reversed: Departure of a relative.

9 of Swords

Regret of choices made and anxiety of choices urgently needed to be made. There's no way out of responsibility.

A. E. Waite's description:

One seated on her couch in lamentation, with the swords over her. She is as one who knows no sorrow which is like unto hers. It is a card of utter desolation.

A. E. Waite's keywords:

An ecclesiastic, a priest; generally, a card of bad omen. Reversed: Good ground for suspicion against a doubtful person.

10 of Swords

Utter defeat, probably because of betrayal. You may suffer, but you're not to blame.

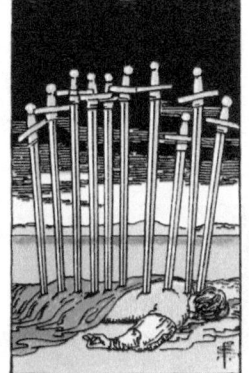

A. E. Waite's description:

A prostrate figure, pierced by all the swords belonging to the card.

A. E. Waite's keywords:

Followed by Ace and King, imprisonment; for girl or wife, treason on the part of friends. Reversed: Victory and consequent fortune for a soldier in war.

Page of Swords

Bravery to the point of being fool-hardy, but there's so much more to win than to lose.

A. E. Waite's description:

A lithe, active figure holds a sword upright in both hands, while in the act of swift walking. He is passing over rugged land, and about his way the clouds are collocated wildly. He is  alert and lithe, looking this way and that, as if an expected enemy might appear at any moment.

A. E. Waite's keywords:

An indiscreet person will pry into the Querent's secrets. Reversed: Astonishing news.

Knight of Swords

Charging right ahead, whether that's wise or not. That's the spirit by which many battles are won – and lost.

A. E. Waite's description:

He is riding in full course, as if scattering his enemies. In the design he is really a prototypical hero of romantic chivalry.

A. E. Waite's keywords:

A soldier, man of arms, satellite, stipendiary; heroic action predicted for soldier. Reversed: Dispute with an imbecile person; for a woman, struggle with a rival, who will be conquered.

Queen of Swords

Mighty power and the knowledge of how to use it. Victorious even without going to battle.

A. E. Waite's description:

Her right hand raises the weapon vertically and the hilt rests on an arm of her royal chair, the left hand is extended, the arm raised, her countenance is severe but chastened; it suggests familiarity with sorrow.

A. E. Waite's keywords:

A widow. Reversed: A bad woman, with ill-will towards the Querent.

King of Swords

The power of what can't be changed, regardless the outcome of battles. Some things one must accept.

A. E. Waite's description:

He sits in judgment, holding the unsheathed sign of his suit. He recalls, of course, the conventional Symbol of justice in the Trumps Major, and he may represent this virtue, but he is rather the power of life and death, in virtue of his office.

A. E. Waite's keywords:

A lawyer, senator, doctor. Reversed: A bad man; also a caution to put an end to a ruinous lawsuit.